Infrastructure Development in Nigeria

This book examines the politics and economics of infrastructure development in Nigeria from Independence in 1960 up to 2015, and the role of good governance in promoting the socioeconomic wellbeing of citizens.

Arguing for the need for transformational leadership in infrastructure development, the chapters examine policy issues and survey the various administrative, economic, and social-political reforms that have impacted infrastructure development in Nigeria. The author also discusses previous national development plans and current Vision 20:2020; challenges to infrastructure development, including corruption; and the future potential of a strong infrastructure network for the economy and citizens. Drawing upon his experience within government departments, as well as existing models of leadership and governance, the author explores the role of infrastructure development in promoting the wellbeing and growth of Nigeria.

Combining theory with practical examples of good governance, this book will be of interest for students and researchers of political science and infrastructure development in Africa.

Michael O. Onolememen holds a PhD in Public Policy & Administration from Walden University, USA. From July 2011 to May 2015, he served as Minister of Works of the Federal Republic of Nigeria. He was also a Member of the National Economic Management Team from 2011 to 2015; and a key member of the national steering committee for the preparation of Nigeria's National Integrated Infrastructure Master Plan (NIIMP) launched in 2015, and was chair of the Transportation Technical Working Group of the NIIMP.

African Governance

9 **African Presidential Republics**
Jean Blondel

10 **Cultural Capital and Prospects for Democracy in Botswana and Ethiopia**
Asafa Jalata

11 **Soldiers and the State in Zimbabwe**
Godfrey Maringira

12 **Islamist Foreign Policy in Sudan**
Between Radicalism and the Search for Survival
Mohammed H. Sharfi

13 **Dimensions of African Statehood**
Everyday Governance and Provision of Public Goods
Randi Solhjell

14 **Destabilising Interventions in Somalia**
Sovereignty Transformations and Subversions
Debora Valentina Malito

15 **Political Protest in Contemporary Kenya**
Change and Continuities
Jacob Mwathi Mati

16 **Infrastructure Development in Nigeria**
A Political and Economic History
Michael O. Onolememen

For more information about this series, please visit: www.routledge.com

Infrastructure Development in Nigeria

A Political and Economic History

Michael O. Onolememen

Routledge
Taylor & Francis Group
LONDON AND NEW YORK

First published 2020 by Routledge

2 Park Square, Milton Park, Abingdon, Oxon OX14 4RN
605 Third Avenue, New York, NY 10017

Routledge is an imprint of the Taylor & Francis Group, an informa business

First issued in paperback 2021

Publisher's Note

The publisher has gone to great lengths to ensure the quality of this reprint but points out that some imperfections in the original copies may be apparent.

British Library Cataloguing-in-Publication Data
A catalogue record for this book is available from the British Library

Library of Congress Cataloging-in-Publication Data
A catalog record has been requested for this book

ISBN: 978-0-367-20107-4 (hbk)

ISBN: 978-1-03-217536-2 (pbk)

DOI: 10.4324/9780367201104

Typeset in Sabon
by codeMantra

About the author

Dr. Michael O. Onolememen was born in Uromi, Nigeria, on September 4 in 1965. He began his early education at Saint Anthony's Primary School, Uromi, and moved on to Annunciation Catholic College, Irrua, Nigeria. He holds a Bachelor of Science degree in Architecture (1985), a Master of Science degree in Architecture (1988), and a Master of Science degree in Construction Management (1991) from Bendel State University, University of Nigeria, and University of Lagos, respectively. He also holds a Doctor of Philosophy (PhD) degree in Public Policy & Administration (2015) from Walden University, Minneapolis, Minnesota, USA. He is an alumnus of the Kennedy School of Government at Harvard University, Massachusetts, USA, where he obtained a Professional Certificate (2014) in Infrastructure in a Market Economy (Public-Private Partnerships in a Changing World).

Dr. Onolememen is a Fellow of the Nigerian Institute of Architects (FNIA), a Fellow of the Nigerian Institute of Management (FNIM), and a knight of the Honored Order of Saint Mulumba (KSM, Nigeria) in the Holy Roman Catholic Church. He has been honored by several professional bodies in Nigeria as Fellow of the Nigerian Society of Engineers (FNSE), Fellow of the Nigerian Institution of Surveyors (FNIS), Fellow of the Nigerian Mining and Geosciences Society (FNMGS), Fellow of the Academy of Entrepreneurial Studies (FAES), and Fellow of the Nigerian Institute of Quantity Surveyors (FNIQS).

In 2000, Dr. Onolememen served as an Executive Member of the Interim Management Committee of the Petroleum (Special) Trust Fund (PTF). This was an infrastructure rehabilitation and development agency of the federal government of Nigeria, and Dr. Onolememen's role was to oversee the Directorate of Projects Management. In January 2007, he was appointed Minister of State for Defence, with the responsibility of overseeing the Nigerian Airforce and all military training institutions in Nigeria. He served in this capacity until the end of President Obasanjo's administration. He was principal consultant in the Nigerian architectural and engineering design firm Gomic Consortium International Limited until June 2011. From July 2011 to May 2015, he served as Minister of Works of the Federal Republic of

Nigeria and oversaw the national roads infrastructure. He was a Member of the National Economic Management Team from 2011 to 2015.

From 2012 to 2015, Dr. Onolememen served as the Chairman, Project Steering Committee, of the Economic Community of West African States (ECOWAS) Regional Highway project (Lagos-Abidjan-Dakar Corridor), constituted by the Presidents and Heads of Government of West African Countries. Between 2012 and 2015, Dr. Onolememen was a key member of the National Steering Committee for the preparation of Nigeria's National Integrated Infrastructure Master Plan (NIIMP) which was launched in March 2015 by President Jonathan, where he also served as the Chairman of the Transportation Technical Working Group. In September 2014, he was honored with one of Nigeria's highest national awards, Commander of the Order of the Niger (CON), by the President of the Federal Republic of Nigeria in appreciation for his meritorious services to the nation. He is happily married to Mrs. Bibian Omonigho Onolememen, and the marriage is blessed with children.

Contents

Contents

Figures

Tables

Acknowledgments

I wish to thank Dr. Greg Uche, a faculty member in the school of management, college of management and technology at Walden University, USA, who encouraged me to write a book based on my PhD dissertation and became one of its earliest editors. I also acknowledge Dr. Robert Levasseur, a faculty member in the school of public policy and administration, college of social and behavioral sciences, and my mentor throughout my doctoral journey at Walden University. He also doubled as supervisor of my doctoral dissertation. I wish to acknowledge Dr. Elizabeth Wallace for her guidance in structuring this book as well as the role she played as its maiden editor. I acknowledge Chief Tony Anenih, who introduced me to public service and without whom I may not have had the opportunity to see the infrastructure development challenges in Nigeria firsthand. I wish to thank Dr. Goodluck Jonathan, Nigeria's President (2010–2015), for appointing me as Minister of Works, with the responsibility of developing policies, programs, and projects in the road transportation sector in Nigeria. This gave me a deep insight into the history of infrastructure development in Nigeria. Finally, I wish to thank my lovely wife, Bibian, and my children, Osose, Osemudiamen, Odalo, and Ehiremen, for their support.

Acknowledgments

1 The historical evolution of Nigeria

Nigeria – a nation in dire need of infrastructure

It hasn't always been called Nigeria. For millions of years, it was just an uninhabited landmass on a planet that had, yet, no boundaries. Gradually, continental drift gave what we now recognize as Africa its unique place in the world. It began to evolve into a place rich in natural resources, plant and animal life.

Then humans appeared. Anthropologists have found evidence that the Nok, a Neolithic and Iron Age civilization, settled in that part of West Africa around 800 BC. Further evidence shows that from the eleventh century onwards, tribal civilization began to emerge on what we now call the Gulf of Guinea, and moved north from there. Differences began to appear that were at first dictated by the heat of the sun, the cold at night, the water, the land and the sources of food.

As the millennia passed, other differences appeared. Languages and customs were established, traditions grew, and people chose appropriate types of shelter, clothing and food. Then the steady development of African culture was interrupted by the arrival of the Portuguese explorers at the end of the fifteenth century, and the brutalities of the slave trade from the sixteenth to the nineteenth centuries. Internal warfare among different kingdoms and ethnic nationalities gave the British the opportunity to establish control of the most economically viable area around Lagos in the 1850s, and to establish protectorates which lasted until 1914.

Then came Nigeria, a country that is now badly in need of infrastructure.

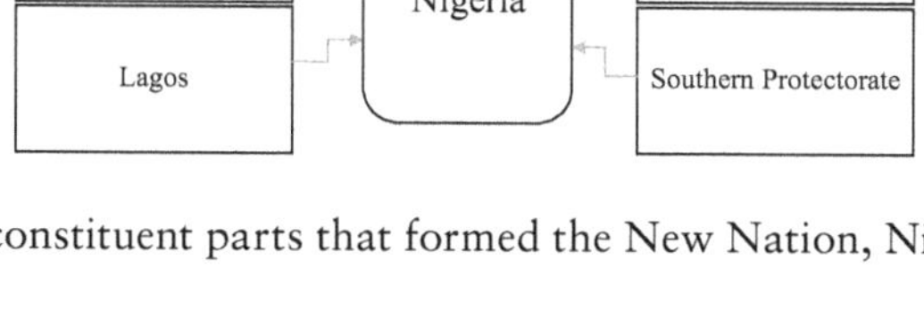

Figure 1.1 The constituent parts that formed the New Nation, Nigeria.

Becoming Nigeria

Nigeria as we know it now, the country that is named after the Niger river that flows through it from north to south, was established over a century ago. It resulted from the coming together of four geo-political areas in Africa. As we will learn, the amalgamations that created Nigeria have resulted in challenges that continue to affect the people today. Those challenges will become evident in later chapters in the book, but first let's look at how the country was formed by the union of Lagos, Niger Territories, and the Northern and Southern Protectorates.

Lagos

Lagos was named by the Portuguese in the fifteenth century. Lagos comprises the mainland, the islands and the city of Lagos, which is the largest urban center in Nigeria and the economic epicenter of the country. Lagos became a British colony in 1861 and was subordinated first to Sierra Leone and then to the Gold Coast. In 1906, Lagos became part of Southern Nigeria and it, in turn, became part of Nigeria in 1914.

Niger territories

In the late nineteenth century, these coastal territories were controlled by a British company that was originally called the United African Company but was renamed the Royal Niger Company in 1886. The territories were divided between Northern and Southern Protectorates in 1900.

Southern Nigeria Protectorate

This protectorate was created in 1900 when part of the Niger Territories merged with the Niger Coast Protectorate and the Oil Rivers Protectorate. In 1906, Lagos was added and the entire region became known as The Colony and Protectorate of Southern Nigeria.

Northern Nigeria Protectorate

In the early 1800s, the major countries in Europe were scrambling for territories in Africa. At the gathering of 1844–1845 called variously the Berlin Conference, the West Africa Conference, or the Congo Conference, the British acquired the territories north of the region. The British protectorate of Northern Nigeria was created to include some of the Niger Territories in 1900.

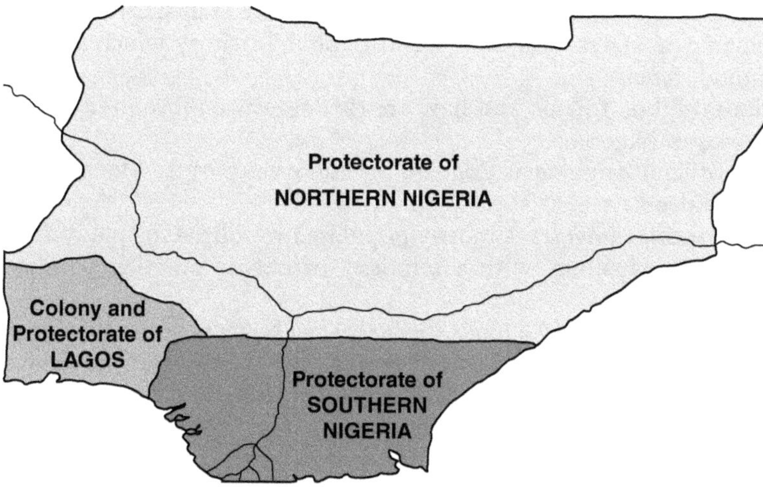

Figure 1.2 Map showing the three Protectorates of Nigeria.

The 1914 amalgamation

In 1914, largely for economic reasons (because the Northern Nigeria Protectorate was suffering financial losses), there was an amalgamation of Southern Nigeria Protectorate and Northern Nigeria Protectorate, into what is now known as Nigeria in 1914. The Colony and Protectorate of Nigeria existed under British rule until 1960, when it gained independence. Several different names were used in the beginning, but by 1963 it had become the Federal Republic of Nigeria.

The purpose of this book is to understand the infrastructure evolution of this republic, but first we need to consider the context. This contextual insight will help us to appreciate what shaped the various leaderships at different times, and how it impacted infrastructure development in Nigeria. Let's begin with 15 facts about Nigeria that will show what the country has become today.

Fifteen facts about Nigeria

1 The Federal Republic of Nigeria is bordered by the countries of Benin to the west, Chad to the north-east, Cameroon on the east, Niger to the north, and the Gulf of Guinea to the south.
2 Nigeria has the largest population in Africa, with about 185 million citizens, making it the seventh largest country by population in the world.

3 It started as 3 protectorates, and later morphed into 2 protectorates, 3 regions, 4 regions, 12 states, 19 states, 21 states, 24 states until it became 36 states, and the Federal Capital Territory which includes the capital, Abuja.
4 Hausa, Igbo, Yoruba and Ijaw are the largest of more than 500 ethnic groups in Nigeria.
5 The official language is English, but there are over 250 local languages and dialects.
6 The south of Nigeria is mostly populated by Christians, and the north is mostly Muslims, with a minority of people practicing indigenous faiths.
7 The coastal city of Lagos is the largest in Nigeria, and saw significant growth as one of the largest centers for trans-Atlantic slave trade from the sixteenth to the nineteenth century. The slave trade forced thousands of able-bodied Nigerians against their will to live in plantations in Brazil, Cuba, Trinidad and parts of the United States until 1833, when the British government prohibited all trade in human beings.
8 Lord Lugard amalgamated the Northern and Southern protectorates and named it Nigeria in 1914. However, the anti-colonial movement became active under the leadership of Herbert Macaulay, who was considered the father of Nigerian nationalism. The independence movement won more and more ground. Names such as Dr. Nnamdi Azikiwe, Chief Obafemi Awolowo, Sir Ahmadu Bello, Chief Anthony Enahoro and Sir Tafawa Balewa are closely associated with Nigeria's independence, which was won on October 1, 1960.
9 In May 1967, the Eastern Region declared independence as a state called the Republic of Biafra, under the leadership of Lt. Colonel Emeka Ojukwu. The Nigerian Civil War began as the official Nigerian government side (dominated by soldiers from the north and west) attacked Biafra (southeastern) on 6 July 1967 at Garkem. The 30-month civil war, with a long siege of Biafra and its isolation from trade and supplies, ended in January 1970. Estimates of the number of dead in the former Eastern Region are between 1 and 3 million people, from warfare, disease, and starvation.
10 The formal education system includes six years of basic elementary schooling, three years of junior secondary education, and three years of senior secondary education. Many schools are over-capacity, and literacy rates among children and adults are higher than the global average.
11 An oil boom began in the 1970s. Nigeria is now the 12th largest producer of petroleum in the world and the 8th largest exporter, and has the 10th largest proven reserves. The country joined OPEC in 1971. Petroleum plays a large role in the Nigerian economy, accounting for

40% of GDP and 80% of government earnings. However, agitation for better resource control in the Niger Delta, its main oil producing region, has led to disruptions in oil production and prevents the country from exporting at 100% capacity.

12 There are three systems of law: Common Law, Customary Law, and Sharia Law. These systems, along with the Supreme Court of Nigeria, attempt to address the pervasive crime and corruption that we will discuss in Chapter 8.

13 Nigeria is a founding member of the African Union and a member of many other international organizations, including the United Nations, the Commonwealth of Nations and OPEC.

14 Nigeria is the 20th largest economy in the world, worth more than $500 billion and $1 trillion in terms of nominal GDP and purchasing power parity respectively. It overtook South Africa to become Africa's largest economy in 2014. The 2013 debt-to-GDP ratio was 11%.

15 Nigeria is considered to be an emerging market by the World Bank. It has been identified as a regional power on the African continent, a middle power in international affairs and has also been identified as an emerging global power. Nigeria is a member of the MINT group of countries, which are widely seen as the globe's next "BRIC-like" economies. It is also listed among the "Next Eleven" economies set to become among the biggest in the world. In its Vision 20:2020 statements, Nigeria has set itself the goal of becoming one of the top 20 most influential nations in the world by the year 2020.

Appreciating Nigeria

The pages of this textbook are filled with descriptions of the challenges that have faced the complex country known to the world as Nigeria. But it's all too easy to focus on Nigeria's trials and tribulations, its bloody history, the ethnic violence, and the parade of leaders who have failed to provide long-term stability. Nigeria also has majestic, remarkable, wonderful attributes that are often overlooked. Let's pause here to appreciate those qualities as we highlight some of the noteworthy features of Nigeria.

Magnificent vistas, remarkable animals and beautiful birds

Nigeria has many natural landmarks and wildlife reserves. Protected areas such as Cross River National Park, Obudu and Yankari National Park, Bauchi have waterfalls, dense rainforests, savanna and rare primate habitats. One of the most recognizable sites is Zuma Rock, a 725 m-tall monolith outside the capital of Abuja that's pictured on the national currency.

Language and ethnicity

Nigeria is a multi-national state comprised of over 500 diverse nationalities and 250 language groups. The best known of these are the Hausa-fulani, living in the northern part of Nigeria, the Yoruba in the south-west, the Ibo in the south-east, the Ijaw and the Edo in the south-south part of Nigeria. Other Nigerian languages and dialets are used alongside English as the official language.

Culture and tradition

Nigeria is a country with rich cultural heritage. 2000-year-old terracotta figurines from Nok and the medieval bronze and ivory sculptures from Benin and Ife are acknowledged masterpieces of classical art.

As diverse as Nigerians are, social life has a unifying effect due to the highly refined system of rules. Marriage, for example, is not consummated between a man and a woman alone, but between the two families. Nigerians who believe in divinities or in Allah may have several wives and adhere to strict hierarchical rules. In some cultures, on the death of the father, the eldest son marries the youngest wife. However, for Nigerians, women are not simply an appendage to male society, rather, they dominate the market place and commerce.

The political history of Nigeria 1960–2015

In this book, the scope is limited to an examination of Nigerian infrastructure development in the years from 1960 to 2015. Some say this is a time in which successive civilian democracies were interrupted by military dictatorships. Others point out that 38 out of the 55 years were military dictatorships, so civilian democracies were just short interludes. A more in-depth look at the history will help you form an opinion.

From colonial rule to independence

Prior to independence from Britain in 1960, Nigeria had limited but functional transportation infrastructure that facilitated economic growth. As a deliberate policy of colonial Britain, railway transportation links were built between 1896 and 1932 linking the north-western commercial city of Kano with the south-western seaport of Lagos, covering well over 1,000 kilometers. Another railway line was erected to connect the north-eastern city of Maiduguri and the southern city of Port Harcourt, spanning about 1,500 kilometers.

Following the end of World War II in 1945, there was an increase in Nigerian nationalism and demands for independence. A Nigerian nationalist movement headed by Herbert Macaulay, and with members like Obafemi Awolowo, Nnamdi Azikiwe, resulted in an intensified call for independence. There was grassroots activism too, led by such people as Mrs. Fumilayo

Ransome-Kuti The British government introduced successive changes in the Nigerian constitution that moved the country toward self-government. On 1st October 1954, the colony became the autonomous Federation of Nigeria. By the middle of the twentieth century, a great wave of people demanding independence was sweeping across Africa. On 27th October 1958, Britain agreed that Nigeria would become an independent state by 1960.

Freedom charter and first democratic government of Nigeria, 1960–1963

1st October 1960 was a remarkable day in Nigeria's history. During independence ceremonies, Princess Alexandra of Kent, the Queen's representative, presented Nigeria's instrument of independence, also known as the Freedom Charter to Sir Abubakar Tafawa Balewa who became Prime Minister. He led an interim coalition government in a British-style parliamentary democracy. This first democratic civilian government of Nigeria was formed between two political parties: The National Council of Nigeria and the Cameroons (NCNC) and the Northern People's Congress (NPC).

However, Nigeria was still not completely free of Britain. The Freedom Charter of 1960 had the effect of establishing Nigeria as an independent constitutional monarchy, along with other nations in the Commonwealth. So, from 1960 to 1963, Elizabeth II was still Queen of Nigeria. The Queen's constitutional role in Nigeria was mostly delegated to the Governor-General of Nigeria, Dr. Nnamdi Azikiwe.

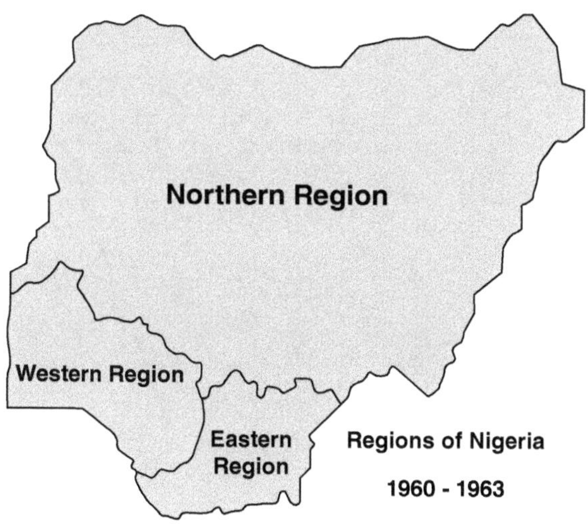

Figure 1.3 Map of Nigeria showing the three regional structure at independence in 1960.

Following the attainment of independence in 1960, the civilian political leadership of Nigeria was faced with several problems such as tribalism, religious intolerance, mutual suspicion between the northern and southern population, and lack of national unity. In addition, the retention of the monarchy was unpopular with Nigerians, and all political parties in Nigeria agreed that the country should be a republic. Nigeria severed its link with the British monarchy, and adopted the President of Nigeria as head of state, on October 1st, 1963.

First Republic of Nigeria, 1963–1966

In 1963, Nigeria became a republic – the first Federal Republic of Nigeria. The politics of this new republic were characterized by regionalism, tribalism, and opportunism. It was a fragile experiment at instituting democracy in a country of enormous diversity and ethnic mistrust. The political parties which were formed along tribal and ethnic affiliations were busy jostling for supremacy and prominence.

Between 1963 and 1966, the political leadership shifted to the Nigerian National Alliance (NNA), an alliance between the NPC and the Nigerian National Democratic Party (NNDP). The political leadership of the first republic was preoccupied with the process of nation building and forming a government of national unity to bring together the numerous tribes and ethnic groups that made up the geo-political entity called Nigeria.

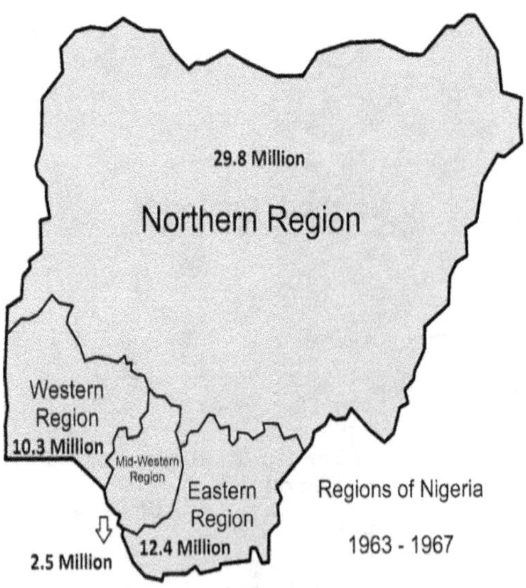

Figure 1.4 Map of Nigeria showing the four-region structure in the First Republic.

The leaders of the first republic inherited from the British colonial administration a country with little or no infrastructure in place. Only a few railway and highway networks were in existence. Water and electricity were not available to the vast majority of the Nigerian population that was predominantly illiterate. The young republic was saddled with several problems that threatened its existence.

The 50th Nigerian Independence Compendium compiled by the Federal Republic of Nigeria identified the numerous issues that contributed to the demise of the first republic as:

- Mutual suspicion and lack of trust between the ethnic-oriented political parties which permeated the socio-political fabrics of the Nigerian public
- Episodes of widespread corruption and election violence all over the nation
- Religious bigotry and ethnic rivalry
- Educational and economic disparities between the north and the south
- British post-colonial interests and agenda

Ethnic and regional antagonism plagued the first republic. Faced with many daunting challenges, its political leadership collapsed in January 1966, when a group of military officers ended the first republic in a bloody coup.

First era of military government 1966–1979

A political crisis in 1966 led to a regime change with the military intervening in the governance of the country. However, that intervention failed to put the political crisis to an end. This was the beginning of an era of military dictatorship in Nigeria that lasted 13 years, and the following are some of the milestones:

- In January 1966, the first military government of Nigeria took over political power under the leadership of General Aguiyi-Ironsi, who although was of south-eastern extraction, was the most senior Nigerian military officer at the time. It only lasted seven months, for several reasons:
- To begin with, there was unrest because of the ethnic coloration of the January 1966 military coup masterminds, who were mostly from the south-eastern part of Nigeria, in contrast to the victims, who were mostly from the northern part of Nigeria.
- This unrest culminated in a counter coup led by officers of northern extraction in July 1966, resulting in the killing of General Aguiyi-Ironsi.
- Aguiyi-Ironsi was replaced by a northern officer, Lt. Col. Yakubu Gowon, who was not the next most senior officer in the military command chain at the time: This singular event led to the erosion of the

> age-long military discipline and values based on command and control, with power flowing from top to bottom in a hierarchical order of ranks. Thus, ethnicity and regionalism found their way into the military and the entire gamut of Nigeria's socio-political system.

The administration of Olusegun Obasanjo lasted four years, and then he handed over power to the civilian administration of Alhaji Shehu Shagari in 1979. Some of the notable programs the military governments implemented included the establishment of the universal primary education (UPE) aimed at providing free basic education to Nigerian children, and the aggressive agricultural program termed, Operation Feed the Nation (OFN). The economic climate of this era was that of abundance and wealth derived from petroleum. According to the Federal Government of Nigeria report (2010), Nigeria became the wealthiest country in Africa during the 1970s with a rapid expansion of petroleum exports, which led to economic growth and prosperity.

Second Nigerian Republic, 1979–1983

Alhaji Shehu Shagari became the president of the federal republic of Nigeria under the banner of the National Party of Nigeria (NPN) on October 1, 1979 after an election that was marred by controversies. For a moment, the political leadership of the second republic was shared between two political parties, the NPN and the Nigerian People's Party (NPP) in a fragile coalition that collapsed almost as soon as it was formed.

It is pertinent to point out that, while the first republic was a parliamentary system of government replicating the colonial British style of leadership and governance, the second republic was a presidential system of government fashioned after the democratic system in the United States. There was a huge expectation among Nigerians that the presidential system of government would eliminate the problems of tribalism, ethnicity, regional allegiance, and religious intolerance that characterized the first republic. What Nigerians wanted so much from the second republic was leadership committed to national unity and good governance.

The construction of infrastructure in the new capital, Abuja took center stage. New universities and tertiary institutions were established. In agriculture, the political leadership initiated a colossal project termed the "Green Revolution". Politicians and a few highly placed Nigerians amassed wealth through political party loyalty.

However, the general public did not experience the benefits of good governance from the leadership. Political conflicts and protests from the other political parties consumed the nation after the results of the general elections that would have re-elected Alhaji Shehu Shagari were widely rejected. Corruption that was the bane of the first republic re-emerged. It was obvious that all the signs were in place for the demise of the second republic.

The Federal Government of Nigeria report (2010) offered the following reasons for the collapse of the second republic:

- The Nigerian economy went into recession after oil prices dropped in 1981, which resulted in diminished economic prosperity.
- High inflation and rising unemployment led to an increase in urban crime rates.
- Poor governance by the political leadership served the interests of a few to the detriment of the majority.
- There was corruption among government officials.
- Massive vote rigging took place in favor of the political party in power.
- Civil unrest, riots and protests arose from a public that was dissatisfied and disgruntled.

The second republic had become as corrupt and chaotic as the first republic. The public dissatisfaction with the political leadership was overwhelming. The nation was drifting dangerously into anarchy. The military concluded it had no other choice than to come to the rescue and take over the political leadership of Nigeria from Shehu Shagari in a 1983 military coup.

Second era of Nigerian military leadership, 1983–1999

Just as in the first era of military rule from 1966 to 1979, the second also saw successive leaders taking power, and it was interrupted by a brief period of civilian leadership:

- 1983–1985: General Muhammadu Buhari
- 1985–1993: General Ibrahim Babangida
- 1993: Brief, unsuccessful period of civil rule
- 1993–1998: General Sani Abacha
- 1998–1999: General Abdulsalami Abubakar

After he took over military leadership from Muhammadu Buhari in 1985, Ibrahim Babangida began an eight-year rule that had a profound effect on the governance of Nigeria. Historians describe it as an era of extreme military despotism, and a period of ambivalence and political deceit. Notably, the leadership indicated it was committed to returning Nigeria to civilian political administration, and the Political Bureau (PB) was set up to plan a viable political future for the nation. Reportedly, there were several coup attempts aimed at toppling the Babangida administration because of his efforts to exclude some segment of the Nigerian society from participating in the electoral process that drew public outrage. However, he did attempt to re-establish civilian rule in 1993.

Third Nigerian Republic of 1993

A presidential election was held 12th June 1993, but the results were annulled when they showed that Chief Moshood Abiola had been elected. In a hurried hand-over of power, a make-shift Interim National Government took over in August, 1993, headed by Ernest Shonekan. The resistance by pro-democracy groups led by the National Democratic Coalition (NADECO), coupled with the unresolved election results, threw the nation into chaos and instability. A few months later, Nigeria was at the brink of another civil crisis.

In November 1993, General Sani Abacha, a serving army officer who was the secretary of defense in the Interim National Government of Ernest Shonekan assumed the political leadership of Nigeria, and once again foisted a military dictatorship on Nigeria. He was known for his brutality and the imprisonment of prominent Nigerians who disagreed with him, including Olusegun Obasanjo, Shehu Musa Yar'Adua, Moshood Abiola and Ken Saro-Wiwa. Abacha unleashed a reign of terror unprecedented in the political history of Nigeria. Bombs were exploding, opponents were murdered, and challengers were harassed and intimidated. The international community led by Britain and the United States isolated the Abacha administration because of its flagrant human rights abuse and lack of respect for the rule of law. Corruption was witnessed at an unprecedented level in the Nigerian political history during the Abacha administration.

The nation heaved a collective sigh of relief when Abacha died in July 1998, and General Abdulsalami Abubakar took over the political leadership of Nigeria, in what can be described as the last military dictatorship. In his determination to return the country to constitutional and democratic governance, General Abubakar initiated a program that culminated in civil rule on 29th May 1999. However, under his one-year administration, corruption continued to haunt the process of governance in Nigeria until power was transferred to the leadership of the fourth republic's democratically elected government.

Fourth Nigerian Republic, 1999–2015

A return to civilian political government occurred in May 1999 with Olusegun Obasanjo regaining power, this time as a retired army General, democratically elected. Between 1999 and 2007, Obasanjo headed the civilian administration under the banner of the People's Democratic Party (PDP). Between 2007 and 2010, Umaru Musa Yar'Adua became the civilian president of the Federal Republic of Nigeria under the umbrella of the PDP, but died a year before the end of his tenure. Following the death of President

Yar'adua, the vice president, Goodluck Jonathan was sworn in as president for the remaining period of the Yar'adua presidency that ended in May 2011. President Jonathan was elected in 2011, and was sworn in for a four-year term on 29th May 2011. He remained in power until 2015.

Summary

The purpose of this first chapter was to set the scene for a discussion of the infrastructure development issues that will be considered in the rest of this book. The chapter began with an overview of the geo-political origins of the country now known as Nigeria, and some facts about the country at present. A detailed breakdown of the political history of the country gives a chronology for the 55-year period, 1960–2015, including the years of military dictatorship and the four republics. Having described the shifts in power during those 55 years, we now move on to look at the concepts and theories of leadership and governance in general, and then as they apply to Nigeria, in particular. As you will see, many experts argue that strong leadership and good governance are essential for the development of a sound infrastructure. Chapter 2 will examine that argument.

Timeline Nigeria: 1960–2015[1]

Although the history of Nigeria stretches back in time, this book only focuses on developments in the 55-year period following independence from Britain. The following is an overview of that period.

1960, October – Independence, with Prime Minister Sir Abubakar Tafawa Balewa leading a coalition government in a British-styled parliamentary democracy.

1966, January – Following years of ethnic tension, Sir Tafawa Balewa was killed in a failed military coup. The most senior Nigerian military officer, Maj-Gen Johnson Aguiyi-Ironsi formed a military government, based on the unitary system of government.

1966, July – General Ironsi was killed in counter-coup, replaced by Lieutenant-Colonel Yakubu Gowon.

1967 – Three eastern states seceded as the Republic of Biafra, sparking bloody civil war.

1970 – Biafran leaders surrendered, and the war ended.

1975 – General Gowon was overthrown by Brigadier Murtala Mohammed, who began the process of moving the federal capital from Lagos to Abuja.

1976, February – General Mohammed was assassinated in failed coup attempt, and Brigadier Olusegun Obasanjo took over.

1979, October – Elections brought Alhaji Shehu Shagari to power in an American-styled presidential democracy.

1983, August – President Shagari was re-elected amid accusations of irregularities in the electioneering process.

1983, December – Maj-Gen Muhammadu Buhari seized power in a bloodless coup.

1985, August – Ibrahim Babangida seized power in a bloodless coup.

1993, June – Military annulled the presidential election when the preliminary results showed a victory by Chief Moshood Abiola.

1993, August – Power was transferred to the Interim National Government with Ernest Shonekan as head.

1993, November – General Sani Abacha seized power and suppressed opposition.

1994 – Moshood Abiola arrested after proclaiming himself president.

1995 – Ken Saro-Wiwa, writer and campaigner against oil industry damage to his Ogoni homeland, was executed following a hasty trial. In protest, the European Union imposed sanctions until 1998 and the Commonwealth suspended Nigeria's membership until 1998.

1998 – Gen Sani Abacha died and was succeeded by Maj-Gen Abdulsalami Abubakar. Moshood Abiola died in custody a month later.

1999 – Parliamentary and presidential elections; Olusegun Obasanjo sworn in as president.

2000 – Adoption of Islamic Sharia law by several northern states in the face of opposition from Christians. Tension over the issue resulted in hundreds of deaths in clashes between Christians and Muslims.

2001 – Tribal war in Benue State, in north-central Nigeria, displaced thousands of people. Troops sent to quash the fighting killed more than 200 unarmed civilians, apparently in retaliation for the abduction and murder of 19 soldiers.

2002, February – About 100 people were killed in Lagos in clashes between Hausas from mainly Islamic north and Yoruba from the predominantly Christian southwest.

2002, November – More than 200 people died in four days of rioting stoked by Muslim anger over the planned Miss World beauty pageant in Abuja in December. The event was relocated to Britain.

2003, April – First civilian-run presidential elections since the end of military rule; Olusegun Obasanjo was elected for a second term with more than 60% of the vote. Opposition parties rejected the result. EU poll observers noted "serious irregularities".

2003, September – Nigeria's first satellite, NigeriaSat-1, launched by a Russian rocket.

2004, May – State of emergency was declared in the north-central Plateau State after more than 200 Muslims were killed in Yelwa in attacks by Christian militia. Revenge attacks were launched by Muslim youths in Kano.

2004, August/September – Deadly clashes between gangs in the south-south oil city of Port Harcourt prompted a strong crackdown by troops. The

Human Rights group Amnesty International reported a death toll of 500, although authorities said about 20 died.

2006, January onwards – Militants in the Niger Delta attacked pipelines and other oil facilities and kidnapped foreign oil workers. The militants demanded more control over the region's oil wealth.

2006, February – More than 100 people were killed when religious violence flared up in Muslim-dominated towns in the north and in the south-eastern city of Onitsha.

2006, April – Helped by record oil prices, Nigeria became the first African nation to pay off its debt to the Paris Club of rich lenders, which had written off two-thirds of the $30bn debt the previous year.

2006, August – Nigeria agreed to cede sovereignty of the disputed Bakassi peninsula to neighbouring Cameroon under the terms of a 2002 International Court of Justice ruling. The transfer took place in 2008.

2007, April – Umaru Yar'Adua of the ruling People's Democratic Party won the presidential election.

2008, September – Militants in the Niger Delta stepped up their attacks on oil installations in response to what they described as unprovoked attacks by the military on their bases.

2009, July – Hundreds died in north-eastern Nigeria after the Boko Haram Islamist movement launched a campaign of violence in a bid to have Sharia law imposed on the entire country. Security forces stormed Boko Haram's stronghold and killed the movement's leader. The government freed the leader of the Niger Delta militant group, Henry Okah, after he accepted an amnesty offer.

2010, May – President Umaru Yar'Adua died after a prolonged illness. Vice-President Goodluck Jonathan, already acting in Yar'Adua's stead, succeeded him.

2011, April – Goodluck Jonathan of the ruling People's Democratic Party won the presidential election.

2015, March – General Muhammadu Buhari of the opposition All People's Congress won the Presidential election.

Note

1 The author appreciates being able to draw on various sources to compile this timeline, with particular thanks to the BBC Nigeria Profile: www.bbc.com/news/world-africa-13951696.

Bibliography

Achebe, C. (1988). *The trouble with Nigeria*. Enugu: Fourth Dimension Publishers.

Adenugba, A. A. (2013). Good governance and accountability in Nigeria's development dilemma. *Mediterranean Journal of Social Sciences, 4*(2). Retrieved from www.mcser.org/journal/index.php/mjss/article/view/267

Adeyeri, S. (2013). Conflicts and political instability in Nigeria: A critical discourse. *International Journal of Advanced Research in Management and Social Sciences,* 2(10), 119–130. Retrieved from www.academia.edu

Ado-Kurawa, G. (2005). *Nigerian politics and national political reforms* (Conference Paper). Lagos: Tellettes Publishing House.

Afegbua, I. A. (2010). Conflicts and political instability in Nigeria: Causes, consequences and prospects. *Journal of Social Science and Public Policy,* 2, 10–18. Retrieved from www.cenresin.org

Bouchat, C. J. (2013). The causes of instability in Nigeria and implications for the United States. Retrieved from www.strategicStudiesInstitute.army.mil/

Federal Government of Nigeria. (2010). The millennium development goals (MDGs) report. Retrieved from www.undp.org

Hague, R. (1992). *Comparative government and politics: An introduction.* London: Macmillan Press.

Ige, B. (1995). *People, politics and politicians of Nigeria (1940–1979).* Ibadan: Heinemann Educational Books (Nigeria) Plc.

Iroghama, P. I. (2012). Trust in government: A note from Nigeria. *International Journal of Academic Research in Economics and Management Sciences,* 2(1), 258–267. Retrieved from http://hrmars.com/admin/pics/857.pdf

Lawal, T., & Oluwatoyin, A. (2011). National development in Nigeria: Issues, challenges and prospects. *Journal of Public Administration and Policy Research, 3*(9), 237–241. Retrieved from www.academicjournals.org

Madueke, C. N. (2008). *The role of leadership in governance: The Nigerian experience* (Doctoral dissertation). Walden University, Minneapolis, MN.

McKinsey Global Institute. (2015). *Nigeria's renewal: Delivery inclusive growth.* Retrieved from www.mckinsey.com/global-themes/middle-east-and-africa/nigerias-renewal-delivering-inclusive-growth

Mustafa, A. R. (2006). Ethnic structure, inequality and governance of the public sector in Nigeria. *United Nations Research Institute for Social Development,* 1–55. Retrieved from www.unrisd.org

Natsa, R. (2015). *Nigeria: As FG launches ATA-SP Phase 1.* All Africa. Retrieved from http://allafrica.com/stories/201503130138.html

Obadan, M. I. (2003). *National development planning and budgeting in Nigeria: Some pertinent issues.* Lagos: Broadway Press Limited.

Ogbeidi, M. M. (2012). Political leadership and corruption in Nigeria since 1960: A socioeconomic analysis. *Journal of Nigerian Studies, 1*(2), 1–25. Retrieved from www.unh.edu/nigerianstudies/articles/Issue2/Political_leadership.pdf

Ogbonna, B. C. (2012). Structural adjustment program (SAP) in Nigeria. An empirical assessment. *Journal of Banking, 6*(1), 19–40. Retrieved from www.academia.edu/

Ojo, E. O. (2012). Leadership crisis and political instability in Nigeria, 1964–1966: The personalities, the parties and the policies. *Global Advanced Research Journal of History, Political Science and International Relation, 1*(1), 6–17. Retrieved from https://www.academia.edu

Okotoni, O. (2001). Problems and prospects of Nigerian bureaucracy. *Journal of Social Sciences, 7*(3), 223–229. Retrieved from http://thescipub.com/jss.toc

Onolememen, M. O. (2015). *The impact of leadership on the governance of infrastructure development in Nigeria* (Doctoral dissertation). Walden University, Minneapolis, MN.

Songi, O. (2008). *Electoral reform in Nigeria: Prospects and challenges.* Retrieved from http//works.bepress.com

Udoka, C. A., & Anyingang, R. A. (2012). The effects of privatization on economic growth on Nigeria: 1979–2007 in retrospect. *International Journal of Economic Development, Research and Investment, 3*(2), 25–35. Retrieved from www.icidr.org/

2 Concepts and realities of leadership, governance, and infrastructure development in Nigeria

The leadership of Nigeria

Having traced the history of Nigeria in the first chapter, our focus should now be on the leadership and governance issues that have affected the country's infrastructure development. The past 55 years of civilian and military administrations have had enormous impact, both positive and negative. We will begin with a brief timeline of Nigerian leaders from 1960 to 2015 (Table 2.1).

Concepts and theories of leadership

To analyze the impact of the Nigerian leaders, we need to understand what the word leader implies. Therefore, it is helpful to see what researchers in the field have said, though definition vary from person to person.

Table 2.1 Nigerian leaders 1960–2015

	List of Nigerian leaders from 1960 to 2015
1	Sir AbubakarTafawaBalewa (October, 1960–January, 1966)
2	General Aguiyi-Ironsi (January, 1966–July 1966)
3	General Yakubu Gowon(July, 1966–July, 1975)
4	General MurtalaMohammed (July, 1975–February, 1976)
5	General OlusegunObasanjo (February, 1976–October, 1979)
6	AlhajiShehuShagari (October, 1979–December, 1983)
7	General MuhammaduBuhari (December, 1983–August, 1985)
8	General Ibrahim Babangida (August, 1985–August, 1993)
9	Chief Ernest Shonekan (August, 1993–November, 1993)
10	General SaniAbacha (November, 1993–June, 1998)
11	General AbdulsalamiAbubakar (June, 1998–May, 1999)
12	Chief OlusegunObasanjo (May, 1999–May, 2007)
13	AlhajiUmaruYaradua (May, 2007–May, 2010)
14	Dr. Goodluck Jonathan (May, 2010–May, 2015)

Note: Out of the 14 different administrations and leaderships in Nigeria from 1960 to 2015, military dictatorship accounted for eight administrations covering a period of 31 years, while democratic governance accounted for six administrations, covering a period of 24 years.

What is a leader?

According to Fiedler and Garcia (1987), a leader is a person who has emerged from a group, through election or appointment, to direct and coordinate the efforts of group members toward set goals. The leader plans, organizes, directs, and supervises the activities of these group members and develops and sustains enough cohesion and motivation among them to keep them together as a functioning unit. A leader marshals and challenges people to transform a vision into a reality. Perhaps the most comprehensive definition of a leader was provided by Winston and Patterson (2006), when they stated:

> A leader is one or more people who selects, equips, trains, and influences one or more followers who have diverse gifts, abilities, and skills, and focuses the followers to the organization's missions and objectives, causing the followers to willingly and enthusiastically expend spiritual, emotional, and physical energy in a concerted coordinated effort, to achieve the organizational mission and objectives.

This definition presents a broad perspective on the concept of a leader. We have examples of leaders of organizations, businesses, and institutions, and, more importantly for this discussion, political leaders. Some people are born to be leaders, endowed with natural leadership skills, and others work hard to acquire the skills required to lead. In the Nigerian context, political leaders emerge through elections that sometimes defy a true democratic process. Some military leaders in Nigeria emerged via violent coups.

Defining leadership

Do leaders always lead? Can you lead without being a leader? What is leadership, exactly? To answer these questions and understand what leadership is, we need to dig a little deeper into the definitions that have been provided.

Northouse (2013) defined leadership as a process in which an individual influences a group of individuals to achieve a common goal. Leadership has two components – a leader and followers. To be a good leader, one must have a thorough understanding of a group of followers and how to lead them to accomplish set goals. Riggio and Murphy (2003) stated that leadership is a process by which a person influences other persons to accomplish an objective and increases the cohesiveness and coherency of an organization.

These definitions identify leadership as a process in which an individual wielding some level of influence brings about the accomplishment or fulfillment of certain objectives. In their definition of leadership, Bass and Bass (2008) stated that transformational leaders motivate their followers to do more than the followers originally intended or thought possible. This type of leader sets challenging expectations and achieves higher standards of performance.

From these perspectives, leadership and leaders are not synonymous but analogous to one another. The inference that can be drawn from the definitions is that while leaders are expected to lead and influence their subordinates, leadership is a process of influencing people towards achieving a clear goal.

Leadership theories have evolved over the years. Two of the leading schools of thought include:

Eight Theories of Leadership – Kendra (2012)

- "great man" theory
- trait theory
- contingency theory
- situational theory
- behavioral theory
- participative theory
- management theory
- relationship theory

Theories of Leadership – Wolinski (2010)

- trait theory
- skills theory
- situational theory
- contingency theory
- path-goal theory
- transformational theory
- transactional theory
- servant leadership theory

There are apparent similarities between these two schools of thought, but there are many more possible classifications. These theories are grounded in one or more of the following three perspectives:

- leadership as a process or relationship
- leadership as a combination of traits or personality characteristics
- leadership as a measure of certain behavior or skills

Fiedler and Garcia (1987) stated that the effectiveness of a leader is predicated on the leadership style that the person exhibits and the extent to which the situation gives the person locus of control and influence over the followers. They identified the following conditions as essential to a leader's success:

- the relationship between the leader and followers
- the structure of the task
- position power

Six theories of leadership

A synthesis of the main theories gives us six key theories as the basis for analyzing Nigerian leadership. These are:

- Trait theory
- Situational theory
- Contingency theory
- Transactional theory
- Servant leadership theory
- Transformational theory

Trait theory

The trait theory of leadership suggests that people are either born or not born with the qualities that predispose them to success in a leadership role. In other words, people inherit certain qualities and traits that make them better suited to leadership. This theory assumes that leaders are born and not made, and that one must inherit the genes required to be a leader. In this regard, the trait theory is analogous to the "great man" theory, which assumes that the capacity for leadership is inherent (Filley & House 1969).

Early studies of leadership focused on identifying the traits of leaders and determining what distinguished one from the other. According to Filley and House (1969), many of the early studies were designed to uncover universal traits, such as intellect and the social, emotional, and physical anatomy of a leader. In Nigerian society, traditional rulers and palace chiefs are selected by the people based on hereditary or ancestral links. The assumption is that certain families are blessed with leadership traits and therefore their successors should become leaders from one generation to another.

Stogdill (1974) conducted two separate scientific studies on the traits of a leader. In the first study, which surveyed a group of leadership traits, he found that an average person in a leadership role differed from an average group member in (a) intelligence, (b) alertness, (c) insight, (d) responsibility, (e) initiative, (f) persistence, (g) self-confidence, and (h) sociability.

At the end of the second study, Stogdill listed ten characteristics of a leader:

a drive for responsibility and task completion
b vigor and persistence in the pursuit of goals
c venturesome and originality in problem solving
d drive to exercise initiative in social situations
e self-confidence and sense of personal identity
f willingness to accept consequences of decisions and actions
g readiness to absorb interpersonal stress
h willingness to tolerate frustration and delay
i ability to influence the behavior of others
j capacity to structure social interaction systems to the task at hand.

Although Stogdill's study clearly showed that there were specific personality traits associated with leadership effectiveness in specific situations, it did not clearly demonstrate what differentiates successful leaders from unsuccessful leaders. Kirkpatrick and Locke (1991) identified six traits that distinguished a leader from non-leader: (a) drive, (b) desire to lead, (c) honesty and integrity, (d) self-confidence, (e) cognitive ability, and (f) knowledge.

While Stogdill (1974) and Kirkpatrick and Locke (1991) pointed out that there were personality traits that differentiate leaders from non-leaders, Wright (1996) argued that other studies found no difference between leaders and followers with respect to these characteristics. As Filley and House (1969) pointed out, if certain characteristics are required for each situation, and characteristics must vary as the situation varies, it is unlikely that the traits required for leadership are widely distributed throughout the population at large.

As such, possession of these traits and characteristics will only differentiate leaders from non-leaders depending on the situation. Filley and House (1969) stated that leadership goes beyond the personal characteristics of a leader and argued that their effectiveness depends on their interaction with the group members; and how well the leader supports and positively impacts on group members to make them better persons and more dedicated followers.

Trait theory and the reality in Nigeria

In Nigeria, four leaders can be analyzed under the trait theory of leadership for their pioneering role in leadership, the struggle for independence, and governance:

- Herbert Macaulay, who started the independence movement in the mid-1950s
- Ahmadu Bello (Premier of Northern Nigeria, 1955–1960)
- Obafemi Awolowo (Premier of Western Nigeria, 1955–1960)
- NnamdiAzikiwe (Premier of Eastern Nigeria, 1955–1960)

Situational theory

Unlike the trait theory, situational theory argues that leadership is a response to situational demands. Proponents of this theory argue that it is situational factors that determine who emerges as a leader. The situational theory of leadership posits that leaders choose the best course of action based on situational variables. Simply put, situational leadership proponents believe that the emergence of a great leader is a derivative of time, place, and circumstance.

According to Hersey and Blanchard (1977), leadership is a dynamic process that varies from situation to situation according to observed changes in leaders, followers, and situation in the environment.

In their situational leadership model, Hersey and Blanchard (1977) name four relationships that impact leadership behaviors in different situations and identity how those behaviors, in turn, affect the perception of leaders as effective or ineffective:

- high task and low relationship
- high task and high relationship
- high relationship and low task
- low relationship and low task

The situational leadership approach demands that leaders vary their behaviors according to the situation in order to surmount the challenges at hand. Proponents of situational leadership theory seek to identify conditions that lead to the emergence of the "strong man", the dictator who appears on the scene following chaotic politics, social and economic distress, and a weakening of traditional government institutions.

Situational Theory and the Reality in Nigeria

Most Nigerian military dictators were situational leaders:

- General Aguiyi Ironsi
- General Yakubu Gowon
- General Murtala Mohammed
- General Olusegun Obasanjo
- General Muhammadu Buhari
- General Ibrahim Babangida
- Chief Ernest Shonekan
- General Sani Abacha
- General Abdusalami Abubakar

Contingency theory

The contingency leadership theory suggests that there is no single way of leading. It is predicated on the principles of situational theory and argues that leadership is defined in terms of the interaction between the leader and variables in the environment. According to Fiedler's contingency theory (1967), the effectiveness of the task-oriented and relationship-oriented leader was largely dependent on the prevailing situation. Leadership is thereby perceived as the exercise of appropriate behavior in a given situation, that will command the loyalty of followers and motivate them to accomplish set goals (Filley & House, 1969).

The performance of the leader depends on the circumstance (Burns, 1978). While most person-situation theorists believe that leaders should adapt to situational demands, Fiedler's research and theory focused on placement of leaders in situations to which they are best suited. No leadership style is best in all situations; rather, success depends on adapting the style to the situation at hand.

Fiedler believes that leaders need to learn how to change a situation so it accords with their leadership orientation. He and Garcia (1987) developed a method to help leaders match their appropriate situations. They then helped these leaders to change their situations or adjust their unique skills.

Contingency theory and the reality in Nigeria

Nigerian leaders who fall under this leadership category include:

- Prime Minister Tafawa Balewa
- President Olusegun Obasanjo

Transactional leadership theory

The transactional leadership theory (Bass, 1985) is characterized by the basic management process of controlling, organizing, and planning for short-term goals. The transactional leader employs motivation through a carrot (reward) and stick (punishment) system. The power of transactional leaders flow from their formal authority and position in the organization's hierarchy. Followers are duty bound to obey the instructions of their leader.

The theory is based on the notion that a leader's job is to create structures that make it abundantly clear what is expected of their followers and the consequences of meeting or not meeting these expectations. The transactional leader resembles the traditional manager (Kouzes & Posner, 1987). According to Bass (1985), this type of leader is most efficient when they develop a mutually reinforcing environment that facilitates exchange with their followers, predicated on contingent reward and management by exception. The exchange between the transactional leader and their followers is intended at helping them to achieve routine performance goals. These exchanges occur in four dimensions:

- **Contingent rewards:** Goals are linked to rewards, expectations are clarified, resources are provided, mutual goals are set, and various forms of rewards for successful performance are indicated. Transactional leaders set specific, measurable, attainable, realistic, and timely (SMART) goals for their followers.
- **Active management by exception:** Monitoring the works of subordinates, watching for deviations from rules and standards, and taking corrective actions to avoid mistakes are the responsibilities of the transactional leader.

- **Passive management by exception:** Transactional leaders intervene only when standards are not met or when performance falls short of expectations. Such interventions may include using the proverbial stick (punishment) to set followers on the right track.
- **Laissez-faire:** An environment in which followers can rely on their own creativity to get the task done is created by the leader. This often leads to lack of direction, with a high probability of not meeting set goals.

Transactional theory and the reality in Nigeria

The Nigerian leader who typified this leadership style was President Shehu Shagari.

Servant leadership theory

Servant leadership has existed for about 2,000 years. The modern servant leadership movement was launched by Greenleaf in 1970 with his classical publication *The servant as leader.* The theory is premised on the assumption that a servant-leader should first be servant. Elements of servant leadership include:

- personal morality and integrity
- enhancing those values in followers
- focus on serving followers
- concern with the success of all stakeholders
- self-reflection

Greenleaf (1977) pointed out that the servant-leader ensures that the highest-priority needs of followers are being served, emphasizing that a leader should be a servant first before aspiring to lead. According to Greenleaf, a servant-leader should possess empathy, foresight, awareness, and persuasion. He believes that servant-leaders are functionally superior because they are closer to the ground – they hear things, see things, know things, and have exceptional intuitive insights.

Greenleaf further argued that the demand for accountability on the part of leadership has deepened its ethical imperative, pointing out that the servant-leadership style is the leadership model that can most adequately respond to this ethical demand. He identified three levels of servant leadership – the servant as leader, the institution as servant, and trustees as servants. He asserted that to improve society, the quality of institutions must be raised to ensure the delivering of institutional mandates of caring for the larger society. He pointed out that trustees of corporations or agencies of governments, have a responsibility to help raise the level of leadership performance of these corporations or agencies, to care effectively for the larger society.

Servant leadership theory and the reality in Nigeria

President Umaru Yaradua was an ardent servant-leader, whose presidency epitomized this leadership theory.

Transformational leadership theory

In transformational leadership, a leader engages followers in a way that raises the level of motivation and morality in both the leader and followers, resulting in expectations being surpassed. Transformational leaders help followers to attain their fullest potential through idealized influence, inspirational motivation, intellectual stimulation, and individualized consideration. According to Bass (1990), good visioning, impression-management, and rhetorical skills are central to transformational leadership. Transformational leaders employ these skills to evoke strong emotions in followers and motivate them to perform beyond expectations.

Transformational leadership describes how leaders can initiate, develop, and implement major changes in organizations, institutions, and governments in order to bring about social change in society. The leaders transform followers through their inspirational nature and charismatic personalities, setting aside rules and regulations, and leveraging instead on group norms and values. This provides a sense of belonging to followers as they easily identify with the leadership and its purpose.

Transformational leadership is deeply rooted in political and governmental leadership (Denhardt, Denhardt, & Aristiguetta, 2002). Public leaders employ transformational leadership to:

- Create a vision for their community, state, or country
- Build the policy agenda
- Mobilize public opinion with respect to policy proposals
- Shape and implement those programs and policies that government undertakes.

Burns (1978) pointed out that transformational leadership is more effective than transactional leadership because, while the latter appeals more to selfish concerns, the former appeals to social values, and this encourages people to collaborate rather than working as individuals. While transformational leaders inspire, provide vision, and stimulate followers intellectually, they tend to be weaker on developing systems, structures, and implementation, which are areas of strong influence for transactional leaders. The two leadership styles can reinforce each other. While transactional leadership can provide for structure and consideration, transformational leadership reinforces it by helping followers transcend their own selfish needs for achievement and self-actualization. Since transformational leadership is a style that deserves attention in the Nigerian context, it is illuminating to examine its attributes.

> **Transformational leadership theory and the reality in Nigeria**
>
> President Goodluck Jonathan adopted this leadership theory as a mantra for his administration.

Attributes of pragmatic, visionary, and transformational leadership

Attributes of transformational leaders include high levels of morality, ethics, and values. These attributes play a dominant role in shaping the quality of leadership and people in government bureaucracy and institutions, and, in conjunction with empathy, awareness, foresight, and persuasion, form the qualities of this style of leadership.

- Morality

  It is vital for the leader to possess personal morality in this case, as it is vital for transforming society and gives the leader a basic sense of right and wrong. This is a virtue that should be acquired by the leader in the formative years as s/he develop from childhood into adolescence, and then adulthood. It is influenced by the values, assumptions, beliefs, and expectations (VABEs) transmitted to the leader during the formative years by parents or through religion, culture, and societal norms, as well as personal experiences.
- Values

  Values are at the core of a leader's personality and what s/he stand for. Values are what matters to someone; they describe who the person is and shape the worldview. They clarify the character of the individual and ultimately the community. Shared values can be likened to the "glue" that binds people together. The relationships between the leader and their followers are shaped by values, and these values represent peoples' rightful claims on organizations, society, and polity. Values clarify the relationship between self-interest and the common good; and help establish a leadership agenda for action. They not only provide a frame of reference that guides the setting of priorities and the determination of right or wrong but also serve as foundations upon which ethical climates in government are premised. While personality is made up of cognitive and behavioral traits, character is made up of values. The leader needs a base of shared values with the followers to function effectively. Transformational leaders and their visions are concerned with moral and end values, such as liberty, equality, and justice. Being strongly convinced about the rightness of their values, this type of leaders help to amplify, elevate, and inculcate these values in their followers, thereby fostering mutual commitment.

- Ethics

  Ethics is closely related to values. It is the outward expression of one's values and can be likened to a moral compass that guides behavior at the individual level as well as in institutional settings. Cognitive schools of thought contend that ethical issues should be a function of either the expected result of an action (consequences ethics) or the application of pertinent rule (duty ethics). Others argue that ethics is much more than following generalized norms, such as consequences or duty. Virtue ethics is more relevant to leadership as it is a more personal, subjective approach to morality than cognitive ethics. It is a way of life and not just a method for analyzing appropriate responses to a situation. It is more relevant to leaders who are intent on transforming society. Virtues are deeply ingrained in the inner lives of leaders, and its attributes such as courage, integrity, humility, reverence, optimism, compassion, and justice help shape not just the way leaders see things but also their behaviors. The demand for more accountability in government and institutions has deepened the ethical imperative of leadership.

- Awareness

  Awareness helps to create insights. Being aware of the current conditions in a nation is the foundation for improving that nation in the future. Awareness creates unusual alertness, and more intense contact with the current situation, to produce intuitive insights during future action. It disturbs the nation's existing equilibrium and awakens the leader's insight as the latter attempts to respond to existing conditions in the quest for better solutions. If, for example, a leader is aware of the perilous state of infrastructure in Nigeria, this awareness should motivate the leader to formulate policies and programs that can address the situation. Those policies and programs should lead to the development of better infrastructure. Awareness helps to create a sense of urgency, which is crucial to societal transformation.

- Foresight

  Foresight is the ability to see the future and project future events. It's the advantage that a true visionary and transformational leader must have, and it serves as a key to transforming people, organizations and society. Foresight enables the leader to foresee what might happen. Examining the nature and assumptions underlying current actions is a necessary step for a leader to develop foresight. A leader with foresight will develop infrastructure that will solve current problems and respond to the demands of the foreseeable future. Leaders with foresight express their insights in the form of vision, which allows them to mentally develop a picture of the desired future. Vision helps in clarifying the direction of change. It serves as a catalyst by motivating followers to take action that serves a common purpose. It also helps to align individuals in the efficient coordination of their actions. When followers buy into a leader's vision, it becomes a shared vision, which helps to foster commitment in the group. The transformational power of a vision can only be tapped into when key stakeholders involved in an enterprise have a mutual understanding of the vision. This understanding can be fostered by persuasion.

- Persuasion

  Accepting a vision of the future is intellectually and emotionally challenging. If a leader wishes to assuage the feelings of followers about envisioned future change, they must be proficient in persuasion. Leadership by persuasion has the virtue of inspiring change by convincing people rather than coercing them. Coercion does not engender trust in followers, and trust is essential if a leader expects followers to act voluntarily. Persuasion helps to build trust between followers and their leader. It is a key element of transformational leadership. Transformational leaders do not exercise power over their followers in the way that authoritarian leaders do; rather, they champion, inspire, and persuade followers to rise above narrow interests and work together for higher goals that are mutually empowering.

Leadership styles

Having reviewed leadership theories, we now move on to discuss leadership styles. Leadership styles have been described in a variety of ways by a variety of experts.

To focus the analysis on Nigerian leadership styles, we will use the three overarching styles identified by Filley and House (1969):

- Authoritarian or autocratic leadership
- Participative or democratic leadership
- Delegative or laissez-faire leadership

Figure 2.1 An overview of leadership styles.

The authoritarian leader

Authoritarian leaders tell their followers what needs to be done, when it should be done, and how it should be done. In this leadership style, leaders provide expectations without first seeking the advice of their followers. According to Filley & House (1969), authoritarian leaders make independent decisions without recourse to group members. In many ways, coercive and bureaucratic leadership styles are authoritarian in nature. The fundamental element of the coercive leadership style is control of people and jobs, with results obtained through direct, explicit, instructions on expectations and demands for compliance from followers. Similarly, bureaucratic leaders insist that subordinates follow procedures and rules.

In the Nigerian context, the political leadership during the military era falls under the authoritarian leadership category. In 1984, when General Muhammadu Buhari took power via a military coup, he introduced military decrees that set the stage for how the country would be governed, without input from citizens or their representatives. His administration's war against indiscipline, for example, made it compulsory for people to queue at transport terminals and public places, including grocery stores. Female citizens were expected to dress and appear in public according to new dress codes decreed by the military regime. This eroded individual liberties and curtailed the freedom that had been enjoyed by citizens in the democratic regime of President Shagari that preceded Buhari's rule.

General Babangida's administration also ruled with military decrees, like other military administrations that held sway at various times in Nigeria. For example, under the Babangida's regime, two political parties were created by military fiat, and Nigerians were forced to join one of the parties against their preference for a multi-party system. The widely acclaimed presidential election of June 12, 1993 was annulled by military fiat when the military sensed that the candidate of the Social Democratic Party (SDP) had won the election and forcefully stopped the final announcement of the result, thus throwing the nation into a political logjam.

The democratic or participative leader

This type of leader forges consensus through participation (Northhouse, 2013) and relies on the functioning of a group or team to achieve results. Subordinates take part in the decision making process, and decisions result from group consensus. Participative leaders encourage group members to participate but retain the final say over the decision making process (Filley & House, 1969). Group members feel engaged in the process and are more motivated and creative. The democratic style tends to foster responsibility, flexibility, and high morale, and because group members are engaged in decision making, there is a tendency for them to be more realistic about what is possible and what is not.

Northhouse (2013) explained that the participative or democratic leadership style is generally the most effective because the democratic leader offers guidance and encourages group members to be part of the leadership process. In the Nigerian context, the civilian democratic political party system reflects the ideals of this type of leadership. The central and regional governments under the civilian democratic administrations of Prime Minister Balewa, as well as the federal, state and local governments under Presidents Shagari, Obasanjo, Yaradua, and Jonathan reflected participative and deliberative leadership style. Major policies of government were deliberated upon by both the executive and the legislative arm, which sometimes organize public hearings, for citizens' inputs in policy formulation and implementation.

Delegative or laissez-faire leaders

The leader who delegates or who is "laissez-faire" offers little or no guidance and leaves the decision making process up to group members (Filley & House, 1969). The leader allows the followers to make the decisions with limited interference in the leadership process. There is a deliberate policy not to influence subordinates, resulting in those subordinates' having a great deal of autonomy and authority. Northhouse (2013) argued that this style tends to be effective only when the team members are highly skilled and knowledgeable in a specific area, and when the goals of the organization are clearly stated and acceptable to both the leader and the followers. However, this style sometimes results in lack of motivation among subordinates, groups, and followers.

In Nigeria, the political leaders at the federal, state, and local government levels usually set up specialized committees to tackle specific issues, such as the national economic management committee, committee on mass transportation, revenue generation committee, and many other ad-hoc committees, depending on the issues the government is attempting to resolve. Such committees are usually given the latitude to make decisions and offer far-reaching recommendations in tandem with the delegative leadership style.

Other leadership styles

Additional leadership styles have been identified, including:

- Command and control leadership style: demands immediate compliance from subordinates; this leadership style is much like the authoritarian leadership style.
- Coaching leadership style: prepares people for the future and places greater emphasis on the education of subordinates, to improve their capabilities and equip them with relevant skills for leadership in the future. A coaching leadership style involves delegating tasks, building skills, and assessing outcomes.

- Visionary leadership style: encourages the mobilization of people toward the realization of a vision.
- Pacesetting leadership style: sets ambitious standards for performance by subordinates.
- Affiliative leadership style: creates harmony and builds emotional bonds.

Different leadership styles may produce different outcomes or results, but, ultimately, a good leader is one that applies any or a combination of styles in a manner and approach that provides direction and motivates people to achieve desired goals. This is a key point to remember as we move on to examine the connection between leadership theories and concepts of good governance.

Defining governance

To understand the impact of leadership on the governance of infrastructure development in Nigeria, we first need to review the meaning of governance. The term is as old as civilization itself; it comprises the process of making and implementing decisions. An interrogation of the concept of governance would reveal that there are formal and informal actors in the process of decision making as well as the process for the implementation of decisions made. Governance refers to the traditions and institutions by which authority in a country is exercised for the common good, and it includes:

a The processes by which those in authority are elected or selected, monitored, and replaced.
b The capacity of the government to effectively manage its resources and implement sound policies.
c The respect of citizens and the state for the institutions that govern economic and social interactions among them.

In Nigeria, government is the dominant actor in governance. In a democratic government, the dominant actors include the elected government, legislature, judiciary, political parties, bureaucrats, etc., while the informal actors include religious leaders, the organized private sector, non-governmental organizations (NGOs), research institutes, media, international donors, multi-national corporations, citizens' groups, etc. However, in a military government, the dominant (formal) actors are the military government that seizes power, military institutions, bureaucrats, etc., while the informal actors include influential businessmen, influential landlords, influential traditional rulers, lobbyists, etc.

> Governance is the exercise of economic, political, and administrative authority to manage a country's affairs at all levels and the means by

which nation states promote social cohesion, integration, and ensure the well-being of their citizens; governance embraces all methods used to distribute power and manage public resources, including infrastructure development. It encompasses the mechanisms, processes, and institutions through which citizens and groups articulate their interests, exercise their legal rights, meet their obligations, and resolve their differences.

(UNDP, 1997)

Eight characteristics of good governance

Governance can be good or bad, depending on the manner and mode of governing. It is good when it allocates and manages resources to respond to collective socio-economic and political problems. Good governance is exemplified by how authority is exercised in institutions and traditions of government, including the process of bringing government into being and holding it accountable. According to the United Nations Economic and Social Commission for Asia and the Pacific (UNESCAP), good governance has eight major characteristics:

1 Participatory
2 Consensus-oriented
3 Accountable
4 Transparent
5 Responsive
6 Effective and efficient
7 Equitable and inclusive
8 Follows the rule of law

Participation can be achieved directly or through legitimate representatives. According to the United Nations (2007), accountability is an important component of good governance, ensuring that those in authority are transparent about their practices. Good governance helps to promote gender equality, sustain the environment, and promote infrastructure development. It also enables citizens to exercise personal freedoms. It reduces corruption and provides tools to reduce poverty, deprivation, fear, and violence.

Theories of governance

Theories of governance have emerged over the years. Toikka (2011) identified the following governance theories: normative, environmental, reflexive, adaptive, and deliberative. The Vienna School of Governance (2012) outlined some additional theories, which include: argumentative, cultural, democratic and legal, network, political, and system transition and transformation. In summary, the following five theories seem to represent the main ideas:

- Deliberative theory:
  Deliberative governance visualizes governance as a process that opens the participatory process of democracy, particularly in relation to language interpretation in the decision making process.
- Argumentative theory
  This governance theory focuses on the constitutive forces and formative conditions for the emergence of government regimes, paying specific attention to arguments in the interpretation of policies and governance.
- Network theory
  This theory includes approaches that investigate patterns of interest intermediation and public and private interactions in the making and implementation of public policies. As Davis (2011) argued, the network theory of governance advances the idea of transformation from government to governance as an important component of contemporary political leadership.
- Transformation and transition theories
  The theories of transformation and transition as they relate to governance share similarities with transformational leadership theory. These two theories explain the process of governance in terms of transition from one political, economic, and administrative order to another.

Leadership and governance: the realities in Nigeria

Leadership is the defining factor that shapes good governance. So far in this chapter, we have explored the concepts and styles of leadership, and theories of governance in general. Now, we turn our attention to the realities of political leadership, which are inextricably connected to good governance or lack thereof. Good governance is the judicious use of resources to solve societal problems. It exists in an environment that is transparent and accountable, and it is a necessary precondition for the development of needed infrastructure in a country.

The transformation and transition theories of governance provide vital tools for explaining the process of decision making and project implementation by both the authoritarian military regimes that controlled a significant portion of Nigerian leadership history and the democratic civilian administrations. It is important that a proper understanding of the problems encountered in the process of governance during the two political leadership eras in Nigeria be closely analyzed to determine their effects on infrastructure development from 1960 to 2015.

The effect of leadership and governance on the Nigerian civil service

Nigeria's history shows that three distinct kinds of political leaderships led the country between 1960 and 2015:

- Colonial administration
- Military administration
- Democratic administration

These three administrations impacted the quality of the Nigerian civil service and the efficiency of the bureaucracy that is saddled with implementing government policies, programs, and projects. The command and control structure of the Nigerian civil service in the three decades of military authoritarianism undermined its heretofore steady growth and prevented it from effectively delivering infrastructure development.

Experts generally agree that the Nigerian civil service was merit-based and responsive to the infrastructure needs of the new nation, between 1960 and the early 1970s, the period following political independence from Britain. At this time, Nigeria practiced the parliamentary system of government for about six years (1960–1966). However, beyond this period, members of the civil service showed evidence of erosion of hitherto held values, standards, and professionalism, necessitating reforms by successive military and civilian administrations.

According to Okonjo-Iweala (2012), the Nigerian civil service became bloated, and its members were poorly skilled and poorly remunerated as political considerations became the purpose for recruiting personnel into the service. Budget decisions by this time, aimed at preserving the bloated bureaucracy rather than investing in infrastructure, as well as delivery improved services to citizens. More than a few citizens asked, "What happened to the once-vibrant, merit-based Nigerian civil service that was inherited from colonial Britain, and nurtured to an enviable position in Africa from 1960 to the early 1970s?"

The Nigerian civil service was further undermined in 1979 with the introduction of the "Federal Character" principle, which set a quota for the number of civil servants to be recruited from each of the states of the Nigerian federation (FRN, 2005) without recourse to job appraisal or fit for purpose analysis. This led to a large and under-skilled workforce, in which employees often did not possess the technical skills needed for the jobs they had been hired to do. This policy entrenched mediocrity and favoritism by placing these above meritocracy.

The role of leadership and governance in stimulating infrastructure development in Nigeria

Leadership and good governance play a major role in the development of any nation; this is particularly so in Nigeria, where the political system is though, federalism, but with an overarching central government that have exclusive rights to the exploitation of natural resources in the country. In such an environment, everything will rise and fall with leadership, especially infrastructure development.

In the over 55 years since Nigeria gained political independence, the nation has experienced a continuous leadership problem, which has resulted in its poor infrastructure. This affects the daily lives and general socio-economic well-being of the entire population, leading citizens to lose trust in their government. They are left to wonder why, despite the huge income the government earned and is still earning from the oil and gas resources alone, basic infrastructure intended to promote economic growth and make life more meaningful are in short supply. Who is to blame? Is it the type of government (military or democratic)? Are the leaders to blame? Or is the leadership style to blame?

A need for transformational leadership

The transformation and transition theories of governance explain the change from civilian democratic government to military authoritarian regime (1966, 1983, 1993) and from military authoritarian regime to civilian democratic government (1979, 1999). These theories aid us in understanding the problems of governance that are involved in such changes. For example, a change in leadership from a background of the rule of law under a democratic government to one of the military draconian regimes, with command and control leadership, and vice-versa are bound to affect infrastructure development in varying degrees. Transformational governance could create an atmosphere of collective vision in both leadership setting, and inspire followers to look beyond their self-interests for the common good of all. The transformational theory of governance is therefore highly relevant in explaining regime changes in Nigeria during the 55 years period when political leadership rotated from military dictatorship to civilian democratic governments, and vice-versa.

The leadership role played by successive Nigerian administrations failed to represent the characteristics of transformational leadership due in part to the military frequently taking over the government with the associated draconian command and control leadership style, which negates the characteristics of good governance, and denying Nigerians the benefits of transformational leadership and governance. Poor leadership and bureaucratic corruption have led to the absence of good governance in Nigeria. In the following chapters, we will consider what changes in leadership and governance might inspire the infrastructure development needed for Nigeria to achieve her development objectives, as encapsulated in the vision 20:2020 development plan.

Summary

This chapter has focused on leaders, leadership, and governance. Theories and concepts have been presented to create a framework for examining leadership and governance in Nigeria. Different theories were presented to illustrate some of the realities that existed under various Nigerian leaders. The argument was made that good governance is essential to sound infrastructure development, and it was suggested that transformational leadership is the best path to future success. In later chapters, we will explore how the leadership and governance between 1960 and 2015 affected Nigeria's infrastructure and had a negative impact on the achievement of the Vision 20:2020 goal.

Bibliography

Adenugba, A. A. (2013). Good governance and accountability in Nigeria's development dilemma. *Mediterranean Journal of Social Sciences, 4*(2). Retrieved from www.mcser.org/journal/index.php/mjss/article/view/267

Avolio, B. J. (2005). *Leadership development in balance: Made or born.* Manhwah, NJ: Lawrence Erlbaum Associates.

Awamleh, R., Evans, J., & Mahate, A. (2005). A test of transformational and transactional leadership styles on employees' satisfaction and performance in the UAE banking sector. *Journal of Comparative International Management, 8*(1), 3–19. Retrieved from http://journals.hil.unb.ca/index.php/JCIM

Baets, W. (2011). Leadership and public governance: Complexity, uncertainty and societal responsibility. Retrieved from http://gsbblogs.uct.ac.za/walterbaets/2011/05/18/leadership-and-public

Bass, B. M. (1981). *The Bass handbook of leadership: Theory, research, & managerial applications* (2nd ed.). New York, NY: Free Press.

Bass, B. M. (1985). *Leadership and performance beyond expectation.* New York, NY: Free Press.

Bass, B. M. (1990). From transactional to transformational leadership: Learning to share the vision. *Organizational Dynamics, 18*(3), 19–31. doi:10.1108/01437730410538671

Bass, B. M., & Avolio, B. J. (1990). Developing transformational leadership: 1992 and beyond. *Journal of European Industrial Training, 14*(5), 231–272. doi:10.1108/03090599010135122

Bass, B. M., & Bass, R. (2008). *The Bass handbook of leadership: Theory, research, & managerial applications* (4th ed.). New York, NY: Free Press.

Bass, B. M., & Roggio, R. E. (2006). *Transformational leadership* (92nd ed.). London Routledge.

Bedell-Avers, H., Angie, E., & Mumford, M. D. (2009). Charismatic, ideological, and pragmatic leaders: An examination of leader-leader interactions. *The Leadership*

Quarterly, 20, 299–315. Retrieved from www.sciencedirect.com/science/article/pii/S1048984309000770

Bryant, S. E. (2003). The role of transformational and transactional leadership in creating, sharing and exploiting organizational knowledge. *Journal of Leadership and Organizational Studies, 9*(4), 32–44. doi:10.1177/107179190300900403

Burns, J. M. (1978). *Leadership*. New York, NY: Harper & Row.

Cheema, G. S. (2005). *Building democratic institutions: Governance reform in developing countries*. New York, NY: Kumarian Press.

Davis, J. S. (2011). *Challenging governance theory: From network to hegemony*. New York, NY: Policy Press.

Deloitte Global Series. (2012). Public governance and accountability. Retrieved from www.deloitte.com

Denhardt, R. B., Denhardt, J. V., & Aristigueta, M. P. (2002). *Managing human behavior in public & nonprofit organizations*. Thousand Oaks, CA: Sage.

Fiedler, F. E. (1967). *A theory of leadership effectiveness*. New York, NY: McGraw-Hill.

Fiedler, F. E., & Garcia, J. E. (1987). *New approaches to effective leadership*. New York, NY: John Wiley.

Filley, A. C., & House, R. J. (1969). *Managerial process and organizational behavior*. Glenview, IL: Scott, Foresman, and Company.

Gardner, J. (1990). *On leadership*. New York, NY: Free Press.

Gardner, J. J. (2006). Transactional, transformational, and transcendent leadership: Metaphors mapping the evolution of the theory and practice of governance. *Leadership Review, 6*, 62–76. Retrieved from www.leadershipreview.org

Greenleaf, R. K. (1977). *Servant leadership: A journey into the nature of legitimate power and greatness*. Mahwah, NJ: Paulist Press.

Hersey, P., & Blanchard, H. (1977). *Management of organizational behavior* (3rd ed.). Cliffs, NJ: Prentice Hall. Kendra, C. (2012). *Leadership theories: 8 major leadership theories*. Retrieved from www.scribd.com/doc/117765913/leadership theories

Kirkpatrick, S., & Locke, E. (1991). Leadership: Do traits matter? *Academy of Management Executive*, 5, 48–60.

Kouzes, J. M., & Posner, B. Z. (1987). *The leadership challenge: How to get extraordinary things done in organizations*. San Francisco, CA: Jossey-Bass.

Kouzes, J. M., & Posner, B. Z. (2002). *The leadership challenge* (3rd ed.). San Francisco, CA: Jossey-Bass.

Madueke, C. N. (2008). *The role of leadership in governance: The Nigerian experience* (Doctoral dissertation). Retrieved from ProQuest Dissertations & Theses Database (UMI No. 3320296).

McLaurin, J., & Al-Amri, M. (2008). Developing an understanding of charismatic and transformational leadership. *Proceedings of the Academy of Organizational Culture, Communication and Conflict, 13*(2), 15–32. Retrieved from Google Scholar

Northouse, P. G. (2013). *Leadership: Theory and practice*. (6th ed.). Thousand Oaks, CA: Sage.

Okonjo-Iweala, N. (2012). *Reforming the unreformable: Lessons from Nigeria*. Cambridge, MA: The MIT Press.

Onolememen, M. O. (2015). The *impact of leadership on the governance of infrastructure development in Nigeria* (Doctoral dissertation). Walden University, Minneapolis, MN.

Riggio, R. E., & Murphy, S. E. (2003). *The future of leadership development*. Mahwah, NJ: Lawrence Erlbaum Associates.

Stogdill, R. M. (1974). *Handbook of leadership*. New York, NY: The Free Press.

Toikka, A. (2011). *Governance theory as a framework for empirical research: A case study of local environmental policy-making in Helsinki, Finland* (Doctoral dissertation). University of Helsinki, Finland.

Vienna School of Governance. (2012). *Theories and concepts of governance*. Retrieved from https://vigo.univie.ac.at/research/theories-and-concepts-of-govrernance/

Winston, B. E., & Patterson, K. (2006). An integrated definition of leadership. *International Journal of Leadership Studies, 1*, 6–66. Retrieved from www.scrip.org/(S(351)mbntvnsjtlaadkposzje))/references

Wolinski, S. (2010). *Leadership theories*. Retrieved from http://managementhelp.org/blogs/leadership/2010/21/leadership-theories

Wright, P. (1996). *Managerial leadership*. London: Routledge.

UNDP. (1997). Reconceptualizing governance. Discussion paper 2, Management Development and Governance.

United Nations. (2007). *Public governance indicators: A literature review*. Retrieved from http://unpan1.un.org

3 Infrastructure development in Nigeria

Policy issues

In the first two chapters, we reviewed milestones in the history of Nigeria's development and listed the leaders of both the military dictatorships and the civil democratic governments that existed between 1960 and 2015. We also considered what we mean by leadership and governance, and learned from experts that good governance is essential for infrastructure development.

From this point on, we will focus on infrastructure itself. First, we will define what we mean by infrastructure; then we can look at the policies that have affected infrastructure development in Nigeria.

Explaining infrastructure

Infrastructure can be defined as a system of resources that can be harnessed for the development of a society. Essentially, this includes telecommunication, energy, transportation, and other public utilities. In a broader sense, the term refers to the full spectrum of facilities that derive from engineering activities for the use and convenience of mankind. Examples include transportation (road, rail, water, and air), water supply and sewage systems, steel plants, electricity, petrochemical complexes, and facilities for information management.

To appreciate the diverse nature of infrastructure, it may be helpful to categorize the possible types of infrastructure. Physical infrastructure includes roads, dams, and railways. Public utilities, on the other hand, covers electricity, pipe-borne water, and sewage. Economic and social infrastructures encompass health and education, hospitals and schools that provide services. However, these divisions are somewhat artificial because people need to experience infrastructure as a comprehensive and well-oiled machine that is beneficial to their health, happiness, and prosperity.

The development of infrastructures is vital to a country's economic growth and prosperity. Proper infrastructure leads to the sustainable use of natural resources. As we learned in earlier chapters, it can also lead to increased productivity, the provision of amenities to enhance quality of life, and a thriving economy. It can therefore be regarded as the foundation of nation building.

Infrastructure in Nigeria

Clearly, infrastructure can be interpreted broadly. However, to make this discussion of Nigerian infrastructure worthwhile, we will focus primarily on the following sectors:

- Transportation
- Power
- Health care
- Irrigation and water supply
- Education
- Telecommunications
- Solid minerals
- Oil and gas
- Seaports
- Government services

It will be helpful to look at the policies of the Nigerian administrations between 1960 and 2015 to determine the impact they had on infrastructure development. Since different leadership styles can have positive or negative effects on infrastructure development, we will need to review the accomplishments of military leaders as well as the leaders of the four democratic republics in Nigeria since it gained independence from Britain. We begin by reviewing the infrastructure put in place by the British colonial administration before the Nigerian Freedom Charter was signed in 1960.

Infrastructure prior to independence from Britain

The infrastructure that the British colonial administration put in place in the 1800s was designed in Britain and aimed at facilitating increased imports from Africa. The rail, water, and road networks that were set up by the British colonialists were used to move agricultural produce, such as cotton, groundnuts, and cocoa, from the north and other parts of Nigeria to the seaports for export, and to move manufactured goods from Britain and elsewhere to various parts of Nigeria, and other parts of Africa. For example, in the period from 1896 to 1932, 1,000 km of railway tracks were laid. These tracks linked the city of Kano in the north to the seaport of Lagos in the south. Another railway line connected the northern city of Maiduguri to the Port-Harcourt seaport, a distance of about 1,500 km. Over time, it became necessary to expand the port facilities at Lagos and Port-Harcourt to accommodate increased shipments from Africa to Britain.

The British also developed other basic infrastructure services, such as electricity in a few major cities, minimal health and education services, and simple communication structures to support the colonial administration. However, beyond these, the colonial administration put no significant infrastructure in place. Portable water and electricity were not available to majority of the Nigerian population, who were predominantly illiterate. It would appear that none of the British infrastructure had been built to last, as it was already showing signs of deterioration in the early 1900s.

Spotlight on leadership style prior to 1960

Colonial leadership style was the default, following the amalgamation of southern and northern protectorates in 1914 by Lord Frederick Lugard, who became the first Governor General of the newly formed country of Nigeria. Employing command and control, coercive and authoritarian leadership styles, Lugard set out to harness the rich agricultural produce of Nigeria and ship the produce to England to provide raw materials needed by their manufacturing industries. Decisions were made independently, without consulting citizens on their objectives, and enforced. Lugard's situational leadership style was high in terms of task and low in terms of relationship. This led to the emergence of independent movements, which began agitations for political independence.

As the move towards independence gained traction, many local Nigerian leaders pointed to the inadequate infrastructure, and the need to build more infrastructure to aid development. Consequently, in 1946, the colonial administrators introduced the Ten-Year Plan of Development and Welfare for 1946–1955 to ensure better utilization of the funds allocated by the British government. The plan was revised for 1951–1955, then extended to include 1960, amid criticism that they were not true plans but rather a series of projects that continued to focus on transportation, communication, and raw agricultural materials. Significantly, oil was found in Nigeria in the mid-1950s, but its impact on the finances of government and well-being of citizens was not felt until the 1970s.

By 1955, it was evident that Nigeria needed to prepare for independence. While the original Ten-Year Plan had been extended to 1960, a National Economic Council (NEC) was convened to coordinate economic development issues. The Council included representatives from local governments, and those leaders were poised to play key roles in the first democratic government.

1960–1963: infrastructure under the first democratic government of Nigeria

Immediately following independence, from 1960 to 1963, Nigeria was a constitutional monarchy as it remained part of the British empire. Nnamdi Azikiwe, one of the nationalists who had pushed for independence, was appointed Governor General to the Queen, a largely ceremonial role. The Nigerian government was formed by two parties: the National Council of Nigeria and the Cameroons (NCNC) and the Northern People's Congress (NPC), with Abubakar Tafawa Balewa acting as the Prime Minister.

There was also significant tension and conflict among Nigeria's ethnic groups. The resulting social unrest constituted a barrier to the kind of good governance that supports infrastructure development. However, there was a move towards development planning that had a broader scope, with the objective of setting national goals for the economy and the general welfare of the population. The NEC, which had been established in 1955, and the representatives of the British government, continued to play a coordinating role. Various government agencies were included in policy discussions, leading to the introduction of the First National Development Plan in 1962. Notably, there was no public participation in the design of the plan. This initial plan and the successive national development plans are described in more details in Chapters 5 and 6.

After the planning was completed, the British representatives began to disengage from administrative duties. However, the Nigerian leaders did not have much experience in administering national plans, nor did some of the citizens who were brought in to take on roles. In addition to the plan's unclear objectives, there was little funding for its implementation and a shortage of skilled leadership. Its chances of success were not great.

Since there were few significant policy changes during this time, the institutions that had been set up under British colonial rule continued to exist and provide some level of infrastructure for Nigeria. For example, the rail system that had been established by the colonial administration to bring agricultural produce from the countryside to the seaports for export was still the backbone of the transportation system, and power stations built in the late 1900s provided basic light and energy to urban centers such as Lagos.

There were a few notable initiatives in the three-year period after independence. The opening of the University of Nigeria in 1960, which Nnamdi Azikiwe had worked on since 1955, represented a milestone in education. In 1962, the Niger Dams Authority (NDA) was created to develop Nigeria's hydro-electricity potential. In the same year, the National Manpower Board (NMB) was set up as one of the earliest signs that employment would receive attention in the future. However, a small group of highly educated Nigerians, abroad and at home were recruited into the civil service by the NMB to play pioneering roles in critical departments of the new independent government. These early policies faced many barriers, such as weak administration and inadequate funding. But there was also increasing unrest and a growing nationalist movement. In 1963, the first true Nigerian republic was established.

Spotlight on leadership style: 1960–1963

Following Independence, Nigeria still practiced parliamentary democracy, modelled after the British political system in which the party leader becomes prime minister after winning majority seats in parliament. Tafawa Balewa, Nigeria's Prime Minister, was a situational leader. As deputy leader of the ruling NPC, he deferred to Sir Ahmadu Bello, leader of the NPC. According to Fiedler's contingency theory, Tafawa Balewa's position was weak and less favorable as the power he had to direct the government and provide reward and punishment was limited. The situation hampered his effectiveness as a leader.

1963–1966: infrastructure policy during the First Republic

Having acted as Governor General since 1960, Nnamdi Azikiwe became the first President of Nigeria in 1963, when the nation became a republic. Meanwhile, Abubakar Tafawa Balewa served as Prime Minister and head of government. The country was structured into three autonomous regions: northern, western and eastern, each with wide-ranging powers and its own constitutions, public services, and marketing boards. A fourth region, the mid-west, was created less than a year later, when ethnic minorities that had been agitated even before independence called for a region of their own.

Although the country adopted a republican political framework like that of the United States, it retained a parliamentary system of government with executive powers exercised by a prime minister. The government was led by the Nigerian National Alliance (NNA), the result of an alliance between the NPC and the Nigerian National Democratic Party (NNDP).

One of the first initiatives during this time was the creation and administration of a Nigerian census. The 1963 census showed that 80.7% of Nigerians were residing in rural communities. As explained previously, most of the infrastructure development under colonial rule had focused on cities, and transportation systems between those cities and the rural communities were in need of attention.

Since poverty was one of the main problems experienced throughout the country, a seven-person commission led by Chief Justice Adeyinka Morgan was set up in 1963. The Morgan Commission considered the structure of the civil service and reviewed wages in every sector, resulting in a recommendation that a minimum wage be introduced. When the government rejected this recommendation, there were national protests, which added to the existing violence and unrest.

Against this backdrop was the double-edged sword of petroleum development. On one hand was the discovery of the Nigerian oil reserves in the 1950s, which meant the potential to bring great wealth to the country. On the other, those oil reserves could not be properly developed for the benefit of the entire country due to the unstable governments of the 1960s and the fact that the country's transportation system could not manage the increased demands in order to carry the oil.

However, it is pertinent to state that this period saw the completion of the following projects, which had been started under the first National Development Plan in 1962:

- Niger Dams Authority, 1962
- Nigerian Security and Minting Company, 1963
- Niger bridge at Onitsha, 1964
- Bacita Sugar mill, 1964
- Port Harcourt Oil Refining Company, 1965
- Jebba paper mill, 1965
- Nigeria Airways
- Nigerian National Shipping Line

In 1965, the Abubakar Tafawa Balewa government made significant strides in infrastructure development by commencing the construction of the 2nd mainland bridge (Eko bridge), financed with a soft loan from the Federal Republic of Germany.

Spotlight on leadership style: 1963–1966

The leadership was visionary and democratic. Structural and economic foundations were laid with clear separation of power between the central and regional governments. Key infrastructures were developed to catalyze economic growth.

The leadership of the first republic attempted to engage in nation building and achieve national unity by bringing together the various ethnic and tribal groups within Nigeria. At the same time, the political parties themselves were caught in a struggle for their own survival, with many people in positions of power pursuing pecuniary interests to the detriment of the common good. This three-year period saw a doomed effort to introduce democracy in a fractured country. In January 1966, a military coup led by Major Kaduna Nzeogu took over political power.

Opening of the Radio Broadcast on 15th January 1966 by Major Kaduna Nzeogu

In the name of the Supreme Council of the Revolution of the Nigerian Armed Forces, I declare martial law over the Northern Provinces of Nigeria. The Constitution is suspended and the regional government and elected assemblies are hereby dissolved.

The aim of the Revolutionary Council is to establish a strong, united and prosperous nation, free from corruption and internal strife. Our method of achieving this is strictly military but we have no doubt that every Nigerian will give us maximum cooperation by assisting the regime and not disturbing the peace during the slight changes that are taking place.

Source: https://waidigbenro.wordpress.com/2016/01/15/how-nzeogwus-1966-coup-changed-nigeria-forever/.

1966–1979: infrastructure development – first era of military rule

January 1966 began with a violent military coup against the leaders of the first republic and politicians, enacted by renegade soldiers led by Major Kaduna Nzeogu. Although the coup was foiled, it produced the first military government in Nigeria under Major-General Johnson Aguiyi-Ironsi, who was the head of the Nigerian military at the time of the coup.

Despite his call for peace, General Aguiyi-Ironsi was overthrown and assassinated in another coup in July 1966. His successor, General Yakubu Gowon, subdivided the four regions in the country into a 12-state structure to foster post-colonial cohesion and streamline administration. He held power until July 1975, when he was overthrown in a bloodless coup by General Murtala Mohammed, who immediately expanded the 12-state administrative structure to 19 states. Six months later, in February 1976, Mohammed was assassinated in a failed coup led by Colonel Dimka. General Olusẹgun Ọbasanjọ then became the nation's leader. Let's consider the infrastructure development under Gowon, Mohammed, and Obasanjo, in turn.

1966–1975: policies of Yakubu Gowon

One of the barriers to infrastructure development was the need to direct funds towards nation building. However, an even greater challenge was the civil war that broke out in July 1967, which followed the secession of the former eastern region led by Colonel Odumegwu Ojukwu from Nigeria and lasted until January 15, 1970. That war, sometimes referred to as the Biafran War, continued for 30 months, resulting in the deaths of about three million people and much general suffering. There was large-scale destruction of infrastructure, such as roads, aerodromes, schools, hospitals, government offices, and residential estates. The new Niger bridge at Onitsha, which had been built by the Tafawa Balewa government in 1964 and provided the main access to the eastern part of Nigeria, was destroyed. The new University of Nigeria, Nsukka, established by the first president, Nnamdi Azikiwe, also suffered the destruction of academic buildings and structures.

After the Biafran War, Gowon's administration repaired the Niger bridge at Onitsha to reconnect the eastern part of the country. He also introduced the Second National Development Plan, 1970–1974, which was an attempt to improve upon the first plan. Input was sought from the public as well as from government agencies, such as the National Manpower Board. Plan priorities included industry, manpower, agriculture, defense, communication, water supply, and expanded social services. In addition, in 1973, the National Electric Power Authority (NEPA) was established after a merger between the Niger Dams Authority (NDA) and the Electricity Corporation of Nigeria (ECN).

Transportation systems grew in response to the demand to move the increasing supply of oil. Two Nigerian National Petroleum Corporation (NNPC) refineries already existed in Port-Harcout and Warri, and in 1974, plans were put in place for a third refinery in Kaduna, in preparation for the anticipated growth of the oil industry.

While the military regime did enact many advances in infrastructure development, there was a corresponding expansion of corrupt practices that grew alarmingly under Gowon. Reports from that time say that there was no attempt to hide the corruption, and all attempts to remove the offenders were thwarted. In addition to corrupt leadership, there were widespread problems in the civil service. Organizations such as the Nigerian Railway Corporation saw growing deficits due to mismanagement of finances. In July 1975, there was a bloodless coup that overthrew Gowon, resulting in a temporary stay on the unbridled corruption.

July 1975–February 1976: Murtala Mohammed

When Mohammed took over in 1975, he was determined to address the corruption that had been a hallmark of Gowon's administration. As the head of state in this next phase of military rule, Mohammed set up an Assets Investigation Panel to publicly investigate the governors that had served under Gowon. In 1976, ten of the twelve governors had their assets confiscated for a total of over N10 million. Mohammed's fight against corruption also took on the civil service. A purge led to the removal of over 10,000 public servants nationwide. However, this did not solve the problems with the bureaucracy.

During this period, the Third National Development Plan was prepared for the years 1975–1980. It was intended to be more ambitious than the second plan, with an emphasis on rural development and the growth of the agricultural sector. No doubt Mohammed appeared serious and would probably have worked to ensure that the plan was implemented without the level of corruption that had become the norm. However, his assassination in February 1976 brought an end to this interlude of anti-corruption policies, and General Olusegun Obasanjo took over as head of the military government.

1976–1979: policies of Olusegun Obasanjo

The four years of Obasanjo's leadership saw many new policy initiatives that directly affected Nigeria's infrastructure, including:

- Universal Primary Education (UPE), which provided free basic education to Nigerian children.
- Operation Feed the Nation (OFN), which focused on agriculture in the country.
- Hosting of the festival of arts and culture (FESTAC) in January 1977; part of the preparations for the festival was the development of infrastructure, such as the biggest housing estate in the then capital city of Lagos (Festac Town), the national arts theater; the national stadium; and the expansion of transportation infrastructure, including roads, rails, air travels, and social services.
- Establishment of the Nigerian National Petroleum Corporation (NNPC) in April 1977 to participate in and regulate Nigeria's petroleum industry, which led to the building and expansion of oil and gas infrastructure.
- Seaport expansion to accommodate the increased flow of oil.
- Murtala Muhammed International Airport, Ikeja – Lagos.
- Dualization of Lagos – Ibadan Expressway.
- Increased focus on road construction and safety, with the result that traffic accidents declined from 53,897 recorded in 1976 to 35,114 in 1981.

These and other developments show that considerable progress was made under the military regime from 1966 to 1979. Perhaps even more remarkable was that, in 1979, Obasanjo peacefully handed power to a newly elected civilian president, Shehu Shagari.

Spotlight on leadership style: 1966–1979

In 1966, the military truncated the republican democratic government that had been established after independence in 1960, which was comprised of federal and regional governments. Instead, the military leadership foisted on the Nigerian people a unitary system of government. Command and control, authoritarian, and coercive leadership styles were adopted for governance throughout the period.

1979–1983: infrastructure policies during the Second Republic

Following the 1979 General Election, Shehu Shagari became the president of a new civilian government. He came into power when Nigeria's economy was booming, thanks to oil production. According to later reports, Nigeria became the wealthiest country in Africa during this time. There was considerable infrastructure development in the new Federal Capital Territory of Abuja, and new universities were established. There was also evidence in the agricultural sector of a "green revolution".

The Energy Commission of Nigeria (ECN) was established in 1979 to strategically plan and coordinate national policies on energy. As part of the plan to lay the foundations for industrial development, the Shagari administration embarked on building the Ajaokuta Steel Complex, Aladja Steel Complex, and three steel rolling mills in Jos, Oshogbo, and Katsina as well as the National Iron Ore Company, Itakpe.

The Ajaokuta Steel Complex had four distinct rolling mills and sits on a 24,000 hectares of prime land bounded by a river. On completion, the Ajaokuta steel company was expected to have a multiplier effect in key sectors of the Nigerian economy, as it was conceived to produce 1,3 million tons of liquid steel yearly, in phase one. It had a built-in capacity to expand to 2.6 million tons of flat iron and steel products in phase two. By phase three, it was expected to produce 5.2 million tons of various steel products, especially heavy plates. Furthermore, the complex had 43 different plants, and was projected to become a major producer of industrial machines, auto-electrical spare parts, as well as materials for ship building, rail-tracks and carriages. The Ajaokuta Steel Complex was to directly engage 10,000 technical staff, plus indirect employment of about 500,000 people.

In the transportation sector, an ambitious metroline project was started in Lagos by the Jakande administration to increase the ability for mass movement of people between the mainland areas and the island due to the huge transportation difficulties in the city caused by perennial traffic jams.

However, along with some revolutionary ideas for infrastructure development, there was revolution of a more alarming kind in places such as the Niger

Delta. While the Nigerian economy at large was expanding, and many leading Nigerians were becoming wealthy, the general population did not experience commensurate benefits. The oil-rich Niger Delta remained impoverished, and there was unrest led by militant youths over the lack of good roads, water, electricity, and schools, despite the booming oil production in the region.

There was also widespread corruption during this period. In a presentation made to US Congress in 2006, Nuhu Ribadu, then Nigeria's anti-corruption czar, painted a bleak picture of what he called "the darkest period" in Nigeria's history of corrupt regimes. He described it as a time of "wanton waste, political thuggery and coercion".

By 1983, world oil prices were declining, Nigerian finances were increasingly strained, and there was ongoing religious and political violence. In a military coup on December 31st, 1983, Shehu Shagari was overthrown, and General Muhammadu Buhari took over as leader of a new military regime.

Spotlight on leadership style: 1979–1983

Democratic and participative leadership styles prevailed during the second republic, with clear separation of powers between the executive arm, the legislative arm, and the judicial arm of government at the federal and state levels. Citizen representatives had a role in the legislative arm and participated in decision making. Accountability processes were established in the execution of programs and projects.

1983 –1999: infrastructure policies under the second era of military rule

The 1983 coup marshaled in the second era of military rule, which saw four leaders: Muhammadu Buhari, Ibrahim Babangida, Sani Abacha, and Abdulsalami Abubakar. This 16-year period was interrupted in 1993 by a short-lived democratically elected government. However, apart from that brief interlude, this era saw significant infrastructure policies, and we can review, in turn, what each of the four military leaders contributed.

1983–1985: policies of Muhammadu Buhari

Buhari set out to follow in the footsteps of earlier anti-corruption initiatives, including the purge of the civil service launched during the short-lived Murtala Mohammed administration of 1975–1976. Buhari was determined to return order to the nation and launched a "war against indiscipline". He began by setting up federal and state military tribunals to investigate the political leaders of the second republic, many of whom were found guilty by military tribunals without having an opportunity to defend themselves.

Although the focus of his administration was on anti-corruption and instilling discipline in citizens, he also took the first steps toward creating the fourth National Development Plan. This was intended, among other goals, to introduce a national transport coordinating commission to ensure that there was investment in developing all types of transportation. Ironically, it was the Buhari military administration that halted the ambitious Lagos metroline project, which held the promise of a model mass transportation system in Nigeria, and the Ajaokuta Steel Complex project, which was to put Nigeria on the global industrialization map on suspicion of corrupt practices that were not proven. In the case of the Lagos metroline project, where the breaking of ground had taken place and construction work already commenced, many believed that it was a missed opportunity to solve the chronic transportation problem in Nigeria's most populous city, after a whopping $450 million loan was secured from France at a concessionary fixed interest rate of 6 percent, for 25 years. Although the project was abandoned, Nigeria still had to pay the loan amount in full.

The "ghost" of the aborted steel projects still haunt Nigeria today, and many believe that this is probably at the root of Nigeria's continued inability to improve industrially. The Buhari administration was overthrown in August 1985, through a palace coup that brought in General Ibrahim Babangida.

1985–1993: policies of Ibrahim Babangida

Babangida took over the leadership of the country at a time the fourth National Development Plan, covering a five-year period, 1986–1990 became ready for launch. He created 11 additional states, raising the number to 30. He did not share his predecessor's approach to fighting corruption. In fact, he reviewed the convictions of many of the governors that had been jailed under the Buhari administration, with sentences ranging from 10 years to over 100, and returned the assets of those who were found to have been erroneously jailed by the draconian military tribunals set up by the Buhari administration.

By 1986, the national debt had risen by billions of naira. The World Bank and International Monetary Fund (IMF) intervened to assist Nigeria in setting up a Structural Adjustment Program (SAP). SAP was viewed as a temporary emergency provision to help the economy for a year or two. But it was soon realized that a longer timeframe was needed to effect the necessary changes in development strategy. The main goal of SAP was to move from centralized, government-run planning to private sector programming.

One of the changes that began in 1990 was a shift from national development plans that lasted only a few years each toward more continuous planning. For the rest of the decade, a "rolling plan" looked towards a 15–20-year horizon and paid close attention to budgeting. Decrees were introduced to expand privatization and commercialization. A national planning commission set up in 1992 was expanded to become the ministry of budget and national planning, and its oversight helped to ensure that planning was less ad-hoc and subject to political influence than it had been under the short-term national development plans.

Although the corrupt practices continued, there were some advancements under Babangida. For example, his government placed a greater focus on rural and agricultural development. Some strides were made in alleviating poverty, guided by the National Directorate for Employment (NDE), which paid attention to rural women and community banks. The Directorate of Mass Mobilization for Social Justice and Economic Recovery (MAMSER) and the Directorate for Food, Roads and Rural Infrastructure (DFRRI) also focused on rural infrastructural development and transformation.

In terms of infrastructure development, the Babangida administration made a significant effort toward building some of the nation's enduring infrastructure projects. These included:

Third mainland bridge, Lagos, which was the longest bridge in Africa at the time
Started the Itakpe-Ajaokuta rail line, to connect the Itakpe steel rolling mill to the Ajaokuta steel complex.
Started the Ajaokuta-Warri rail line, to link the Ajaokuta steel complex to the steel company in Aladja, as well as Warri seaport.
commenced he Aluminium smelter plant in Ikot-Abasi.
The International Conference Centre, Abuja
The Federal Secretariat Complex, Abuja
The National Assembly Complex, Abuja
The Presidential villa, Abuja
The Supreme Court Complex, Abuja
Abuja International Airport
Massive development of key infrastructure in the new federal capital city of Abuja

When he took over in 1985, Babangida committed to ceding power to a civilian government in 1990, but he failed to honor his pledge. However, due to political unrest following the annulment of the presidential election of June 12, 1993, presumably won by Moshood Abiola of the Social Democratic Party (SDP), Babangida stepped aside. He was replaced by an unelected interim civilian government, headed by Chief Ernest Shonekan. Members of the interim government were handpicked by the Babangida's administration. This arrangement proved to be weak in the face of the struggle for the actualization of the June 12, 1993 election victory of Abiola by pro-democracy groups that included the Nigerian Labour Congress.

1993: Third Republic of Nigeria

During this brief period between military leaders, little attention was paid to developing new infrastructure policy.

1993–1998: policies of Sani Abacha

The weak third republic was overthrown in a coup that brought General Sani Abacha to power as Nigeria's next military leader. Although he initiated an investigation of corruption and excessive spending during the Babangida administration, Abacha himself was not any better. He opposed the efforts of the War Against Indiscipline and Corruption (WAI-C). After his death, his family was found to have benefitted from illegally obtained funds.

Abacha has been described as one of the most corrupt leaders of this period; billions of dollars that were intended for development were diverted to Abacha and his cronies. After his regime, enormous amounts of money were retrieved from his family (Adoke, 2019). Government agencies that had been set up to help with the smooth running of infrastructure projects, or to assist with aiding the poor in rural areas, were unable to function properly during his reign. Major governmental companies, such as Nigeria Airways, Nigerian National Shipping Line, the oil refineries, and the steel rolling mills, all suffered, along with the education sector. Profits from the oil industry were illegally diverted. Corruption was legitimized.

Abacha used coercion to convince his ministers and other government officials to take on infrastructure projects, and, even in the face of corrupt practices. Some of those projects were completed. For example, the Petroleum [Special] Trust Fund (PTF) was formed to use profits from oil to fund the rehabilitation of urban and rural roads, transportation, educational and health institution infrastructure, urban water supply schemes, and irrigation projects. Abacha introduced the federal character principle, a system of quota imposed on government policies and programs. He also restructured the state and local governments, and created six additional states, expanding the number to 36.

Most noteworthy was the introduction of the Vision 2010 program, which promoted forward thinking across all sectors of the economy. However, in 1998, Abacha died under mysterious circumstances. The official announcement was that he died of a heart attack; foul play was suspected but never proved. Leadership passed to Abdulsalami Abubakar.

1998–1999: policies of Abdulsalami Abubakar

Although he was an experienced military officer, a few days after he came into power, he committed to holding an election within a year to transfer power to a civilian government. He oversaw the writing of a new constitution, and set up the Independent National Electoral Commission (INEC), which organized local, state, and national elections leading to handing over of power to an elected government on May 29, 1999.

Abubakar was not completely free from allegations of corruption, and there were criticisms from foreign observers that the elections he held were not fair. However, he did complete a process that resulted in a peaceful transfer of power to the fourth republic, ending 16 years of military rule. During his year in office, Abubakar made little impact on infrastructure development, perhaps due to the short tenure of his administration. By ensuring the return to a civilian administration, he set the scene for future leaders to continue the work of building Nigeria.

Spotlight on leadership style: 1983–1999

Authoritarian and dictatorial leadership styles guided this second era of military administration. Under military dictatorships, government plans and projects are often implemented more quickly than they are in civilian democratic administrations due to the authoritarian nature of military regimes with inherent absolute powers. However, accountability and corruption become thorny issues under such totalitarian regimes, especially as experienced in the second era of military rule in Nigeria. Seventeen additional states and hundreds of new local government areas were created by military fiat.

1999–2015: Fourth Nigerian Republic

Nigeria returned to civilian rule with presidential elections and a new constitution in 1999, signaling the birth of the fourth republic. The 1999 constitution has many similarities to the US constitution, and its National Assembly (Legislature) shares many of the functional components of US Congress. Nigeria is a federal republic, with an elected bicameral National Assembly composed of a Senate and a House of Representatives. Its three branches are the legislature, executive, and judiciary, and its three tiers of government are the federal, state, and local governments.

Between 1999 and 2015, there were three democratically elected presidents: Olusegun Obasanjo, Umaru Yar'Adua, and Goodluck Jonathan, whose tenures we will now examine for progress in infrastructure development.

1999–2007: Olusegun Obasanjo

On May 29, 1999, after a prolonged era of military dictatorship, the fourth republic was established with former military leader, retired General

Obasanjo, serving as the democratic leader of Nigeria. It is important to stress that Obasanjo is the first person in the history of Nigeria to hold power twice, first as military leader and later as civilian leader. President Obasanjo's election under the banner of the People's Democratic Party (PDP) marked the end of 16 years of military rule. His first administration lasted from 1999 to 2003 and focused on achieving stability, fighting corruption, and building the democratic process.

One of the policies already in place was the Vision 2010 plan of Sani Abacha, launched during the military era. However, Obasanjo was a critic of Abacha, and he terminated the Vision 2010 Agenda.

Instead of Vision 2010, the new democratic administration immediately initiated a four-year plan: the National Economic Direction, 1999–2003. As a result, work began on many significant infrastructure projects. There was a focus on rehabilitating the neglected and decaying power infrastructure. Beyond this, attention was paid to building the country's telecommunication infrastructure with the establishment of the General System of Mobile (GSM) telephoning services in order to augment the system in Nigeria, which, before now, had relied greatly on limited land line telephone infrastructure. The Obasanjo administration recorded enormous success in the GSM telephoning.

Obasanjo made several attempts to institute positive governance. The Federal Government of Nigeria (2010) report stated that under this government, Nigeria's international image and reputation, which had been tarnished by the long military dictatorships, improved. The government wanted to position Nigeria as a leader in fostering democracy and economic growth, both within its own borders and across Africa. The West African subcontinent, as well as South Africa, benefitted from an enhanced economic relationship with Nigeria because of the Obasanjo administration's policies. Perhaps the most prominent legacy of this administration is its efforts to eradicate corruption from Nigeria. The Obasanjo administration established the Independent Corrupt Practices Commission (ICPC) in 2000 and the Economic and Financial Crimes Commission (EFCC) in 2003 to prosecute government and public officials for corruption, and to recover stolen funds from public servants. This was adjudged by many as a landmark government policy and an act of good governance.

Nigeria enjoyed relative peace and tranquility under the Obasanjo administration. His preventing another military dictatorship in Nigeria has been acclaimed as a huge accomplishment. The economic policies of his administration were remarkable and included the reform of the telecommunication sector, which resulted in the introduction of a wireless telephone system in Nigeria. The poverty alleviation program was also established, with the aim of eradicating poverty and improving the quality of life for rural people. The long list of accomplishments made by the Obasanjo administration attests to credible elements of good governance in political leadership in Nigeria. It is noteworthy that Obasanjo was the first democratically elected leader in the history of the country's politics to cede power peacefully to an elected civilian administration. He did so in 2007.

Obasanjo's second administration began with the inauguration of Nigeria's 5th National Assembly in May 1999. This consisted of 109 senators and 360 representatives of constituencies nationwide. The National Assembly set up committees, many of which focused on the infrastructure sector, including health, housing, water, agriculture, education, the environment, women and youth, as well as power. An important policy move was the introduction of the National Economic Empowerment and Development Strategy (NEEDS), which operated at the federal level, while the State Economic Empowerment and Development Strategies (SEEDS) were prepared by all 36 Nigerian states and the Federal Capital Territory (FCT). Wealth creation and anti-poverty programs through private sector development were emphasized by the NEEDS program. The Infrastructure Concession and Regulatory Commission Act (ICRC) was established to regulate public-private partnerships in infrastructure development.

President Obasanjo took a personal interest in the Nigerian oil and gas sector, and was one of the first signatories on the new international Extractive Industries Transparency Initiative (EITI) launched in 2003. One of its first tasks was to conduct an audit of the oil and gas sector from 1999 to 2004. While the official production records showed that most of the oil revenues were properly accounted for, there were also indications that data were not being properly gathered, and there were unaccounted-for losses. The Nigerian EITI recommended revisions to improve record-keeping as one anti-corruption strategy.

Obasanjo's government launched many infrastructure programs, despite the huge amount of debt that he inherited. Based on his ambitious reform agenda, in September 2005, the Paris Club granted Nigeria debt relief of $18 billion. The Obasanjo administration ensured that debt relief expenditures were dedicated to projects and programs that benefited the country. To ensure accountability in the utilization of debt relief funds, a project management team was set up to monitor initiatives and projects arising from Nigeria's receipt of debt relief in 2005.

In summary, the eight years of Obasanjo's administration resulted in several new policies and many innovative programs which advanced infrastructure development, such as:

- Universal Basic Education.
- The Independent Corrupt Practices & Other Related Offences Commission.
- Economic and Financial Crimes Commission.
- National Economic Empowerment and Development Strategy.
- State Economic Empowerment and Development Strategy.

- Local Economic and Development Strategy.
- Millennium Development Goals (MDGs) based on the United Nations anti-poverty targets.
- Infrastructure Concession and Regulatory Commission Act to oversee public-private partnership infrastructure development programs.
- Due Process Policy (DPP), intended to make government and private sector businesses abide by established rules and procedures.
- National Integrated Power Project (NIPP). Some existing plants were refurbished, which would have increased the country's capacity to about 10,000 megawatts of electricity generation. In addition, the reform intended to separate privatized power into three distinct mandates: generation, transmission, and distribution.
- The recapitalization policy aimed at strengthening banks and other financial institutions.
- A robust foreign policy aimed at repackaging Nigeria's diplomatic image and disengaging the country from an excessive and detrimental Afro-centric policy.
- Successful recovery of stolen money from corrupt public officers.
- Providing leadership in the restoration of peace and democracy in the two West African countries of Sierra Leone and Liberia.
- A pension reform scheme, which led to the emergence of a credible public and private pension scheme.
- Niger Delta Development Commission.

2007–2010: Umaru Yar'Adua

At the end of the Obasanjo administration, and after an electoral process in Nigeria that was declared free and fair for the first time by international observers, Umaru Musa Yar'Adua became the second civilian political leader in the fourth republic under the banner of the PDP. He held power between 2007 and 2010, when he died in office of natural causes. His government's objectives were commendable, and it is unfortunate that his political leadership lasted for only three years.

Yar'Adua's administration was, for all intents and purposes, an extension of the Obasanjo administration. Its policies and programs were directed at target areas of governance. Yar'Adua articulated a program, "the seven-point agenda", as the cardinal program of his administration. This was a development policy initiative that included the following:

- Introduction of an infrastructure development policy, which proposed a radical and massive rural and urban transformation: the resuscitation of the ailing infrastructure; the construction of new roads, railroads, seaport and airport facilities; upgrading and expansion of existing

infrastructures; and the provision of such basic social amenities as water and electricity.
- Reforming the energy sector of the Nigerian economy to increase electricity production to the projected 10,000 megawatts output, and enhancing oil and gas production.
- Confronting and addressing the social unrest and militancy in the oil-producing Niger Delta region through the provision of infrastructures and amenities, poverty reduction, and wealth redistribution. He also granted pardon to repentant militants under the "Amnesty" program of his administration.
- Transforming the public health sector by building more health facilities across the country to fight epidemic and pandemic diseases, as well as reducing maternal and infant mortality.
- Revolutionizing the educational system by transforming the tertiary institutions and making education affordable.
- Pursuing a zero-tolerance policy for corruption, probity, accountability, and transparency.
- Reducing unemployment through the creation of jobs in the public and private sectors.

2010–2015: Goodluck Jonathan

After the death of Yar'Adua, Vice-President Goodluck Jonathan was sworn in as president to serve out the unexpired year of the Yar'Adua administration, in accordance with Nigeria's constitution. In April 2011, Jonathan won the presidential election under the platform of the PDP. Although he continued most of his predecessor's work, he quickly launched his own administration's development blueprint, the "transformation agenda", which aimed at transforming the economy and improving the well-being of all Nigerians.

The Jonathan administration carried out fundamental reforms and policy changes to achieve its strategic economic goal of becoming one of the top 20 economies in the world by 2020. Four years after the launch of the transformation agenda document, Nigeria became the largest economy in Africa. The achievements of the Jonathan administration included:

- The local content policy in the oil and gas sector, which increased indigenous participation in the oil and gas industry and created linkages to other sectors of the economy, leading to more jobs for Nigerians in that sector.
- The freedom of information (FOI) Act, which improved the transparency of government activities and made public records and information more accessible.

- Reforming the transportation sector by strengthening the legal framework for private sector participation, leading to the construction of landmark infrastructure projects, including the construction of two new bridges: the new river Benue bridge in Loko/Oweto, linking the north to the south, and the second river Niger bridge in Onitsha/Asaba, linking the east to the west; the dualization and rehabilitation of major north-south and east-west arterial roads; the completion of the construction of the Nigeria-Cameroon segment of the Trans-African highway project; and the construction of a new national network for standard gauge speed-train services for the two existing north-south narrow-gauge lines inherited from the colonial administration in 1960, completing the Abuja-Kaduna new standard-gauge rail line segment and initiating the construction of a new standard gauge east-west rail line from Calabar to Lagos, with an extension to the commercial city of Onitsha.
- The "national integrated infrastructure master plan", which is a blueprint for expanding and modernizing the nation's infrastructure over the next 30 years.
- Ending government participation in the production and distribution of fertilizer and seeds, and developing value chains in agricultural priority areas, such as rice, cassava, livestock, and fisheries, resulting in increased farmer's access to inputs and expanded domestic production of fertilizer as well as bringing down the food importation bill from 1.4 trillion naira in 2009 to 684 billion naira by December 2013.
- The launching of the National Industrial Revolution Plan, aimed at driving agro-allied and processing industries, and light manufacturing.
- The launching of the National Automotive Policy, which aimed to establish five new vehicle assembling plants,
- Initiating the Nigerian development bank for improved access to long-term finance for the development program.
- Establishment of the sovereign wealth fund, to provide enough buffers in times of economic crises.
- Introduction of the treasury single account (TSA) in 2012 to unify the structure of the government bank account, leading to better management of government's cash flow.
- The introduction of the Integrated Payroll System (IPPIS), which tackled the problem of ghost workers and curtailed rising recurrent expenditure, leading to the discovery of 60,450 ghost workers in the federal government and yielding savings of about 185 billion naira.
- The cashless policy aimed at developing and modernizing the Nigerian payment system, thereby limiting the adverse effects of a largely cash-based society.
- Enforcement of compliance with the Nigerian uniform bank account number code, leading to a reduction in the cost of transactions and the ability to track illicit funds.

Despite the successes recorded by the Jonathan administration, the looming threat of the Boko Haram terrorist group with its associated mass killings, kidnapping of innocent Nigerians, especially the case of the 219 Chibok school girls who were abducted in April 2014 from their hostels in the middle of the night, represented a low point in the administration. It is worth noting that Boko Haram predated the Jonathan administration, having emerged as far back as 2002. The group, however, became extremely malignant after the murder of its founding leader, Mohammed Yusuf, in July 2009 by government security operatives.

Although the Jonathan administration overhauled the nation's security architecture and re-equipped its security apparatus, leading to the killing of members of the Boko Haram terrorist group by government forces, and making it possible to conduct the 2015 elections in the north-eastern part of Nigeria, the group was not fully defeated before the end of the Jonathan administration by May 2015. The Jonathan administration's reforms consolidated Nigeria's economic growth and stability, generating private sector investments in infrastructure that supported growth in the real sectors of the economy. The innovations also saw the nation becoming the largest economy in Africa in terms of the GDP, which stood at almost 500 billion dollars in 2013, and placed it as one of the fastest-growing economies in the world by 2015.

Spotlight on leadership style: 1999–2015

The leadership style in the fourth republic was participative democratic leadership, in which citizens weigh in on proposed policies via public hearings and participate in workshops aimed at developing policies and the implementation of plans for major government policies and programs. The leadership was premised on high task and high relationship activities, and has been successful in positioning Nigeria as a leader in the promotion of democracy and economic growth in Africa.

Summary

This third chapter traced the history of infrastructure policy from 1960 to 2015 under successive Nigerian leaders. This history shows that the country was subject to democratic leadership, military rule, and civil war during this period. All the political events and policy decisions had dire effects on Nigeria's infrastructure development. In particular, a spotlight was placed on the leadership style under each distinct regime, and its impact on infrastructure policy, in order to explain the impact of leadership in preparation for further analysis.

Bibliography

Adenugba, A. A. (2013). Good governance and accountability in Nigeria's development dilemma. *Mediterranean Journal of Social Sciences, 4*(2). Retrieved from www.mcser.org/journal/index.php/mjss/article/view/267

Adoke, M. B. (2019). Burden of service: Reminiscenes of Nigeria's former Attorney-General (1st ed.). London: Clint Street Publishing.

Akinwale, A. A. (2010). The menace of inadequate infrastructure in Nigeria. *African Journal of Science, Technology, Innovation and Development, 2*(3), 207–228. Retrieved from www.ajstid.com

Cheema, G. S. (2005). *Building democratic institutions: Governance reform in developing countries.* New York, NY: Kumarian Press.

Federal Government of Nigeria. (2010). The millennium development goals (MDGs) report. Retrieved from www.undp.org/content/dam/undp/libray/MDG/english/MDG

Gwilliam, K. (2011). *Africa's transport infrastructure: Mainstreaming maintenance and management.* Washington, DC: The World Bank.

Hawkins, J. (2013). *How to note: Reducing corruption in infrastructure sector.* Conference Paper.

Ige, B. (1995). *People, politics and politicians of Nigeria (1940–1979).* Ibadan: Heinemann Educational Books (Nigeria) Plc. No access.

Iroghama, P. I. (2012). Trust in government: A note from Nigeria. *International Journal of Academic Research in Economics and Management Sciences, 2*(1), 258–267. Retrieved from http://hrmars.com/admin/pics/857.pdf

Jonathan, G. (2015). *Innovative reforms of President Goodluck Jonathan's administration* (pp. 17–24). Abuja: The Office of the Chief Economic Adviser to the President.

Kemp, R., Parto, S., & Gibson, R. B. (2005). Governance for sustainable development: Moving from theory to practice. *International Journal of Sustainable Development, 8*(1/2), 12–30. doi:10.1504/IJSD.2005.007372

Lawal, T., & Oluwatoyin, A. (2011). National development in Nigeria: Issues, challenges and prospects. *Journal of Public Administration and Policy Research, 3*(9), 237–241. Retrieved from www.academicjournals.org

Marcellus, I. C. (2009). Development planning in Nigeria: Reflections on the national economic empowerment and development strategies (NEEDS) 2003–2007. *Journal of Social Sciences, 20*(30), 197–210.

Mbanefo, C. A. (2000). The role of engineering infrastructure in national development. In M. D. Abdullahi (Ed.), *Provision & maintenance of engineering infrastructure for technological development in Nigeria* (pp. 37–44). Kaduna: Fahimta Publishing Company.

Mohammed, K., Chapola, D., & Bello, A. (2013). The state of Nigerian economy in the 21st century: Privatization and commercialization programs under Obasanjo-Atiku regime. *European Scientific Journal, 9*(19), 88–98. Retrieved from http://eujournal.org/index.php/esj/

Ogu, V. I. (2000). Stakeholders' partnership approach to infrastructure provision and management in developing world cities: Lessons from the sustainable Ibadan project. *Human Settlement Development, 111*, 1–18. doi:10.1016/S0197–3975(00)00015-1

Ojo, E. O. (2012). Leadership crisis and political instability in Nigeria, 1964–1966: The personalities, the parties and the policies. *Global Advanced Research Journal of History, Political Science and International Relation*, *1*(1), 6–17. Retrieved from http://garj.org/garjhpsir/pdf/2012/feb/Ojo.pdf

Onolememen, M. O. (2015). *The impact of leadership on the governance of infrastructure development in Nigeria* (Doctoral dissertation). Walden University, Minneapolis, MN.

4 Reforms and infrastructure development

Reforms in Nigeria

As we discussed in the previous chapters, the political leaders of Nigeria have initiated and implemented various economic, political, and social policies and reforms. From this point on, we will explore the ways in which those leaders and reforms affected infrastructure development in the country. The question that will be considered in this chapter is:

> How did the reforms of the different political eras affect the development of infrastructure in Nigeria between 1960 and 2015?

The reforms initiated during the period from 1960 to 2015 can be broadly divided into three categories:

a Socio-political reform
b Economic reform
c Administrative reform

Socio-political reform

In 1960, Nigeria inherited a parliamentary political system of government from colonial Britain. The system was fashioned after the British system, with the Queen of England acting as the titular head of government and a prime minister in charge of its day-to-day operation. This system was strange to the political leaders in Nigeria, who had little or no knowledge of the parliamentary system of government. Following independence in 1960, Tafawa Balewa emerged as the first prime minister of Nigeria under the parliamentary system, with Nnamdi Azikiwe acting as president (without executive power).

The three regional governments enjoyed autonomy, with Ahmadu Bello as premier of the northern region, Obafemi Awolowo as premier of the western region, and Michael Okpara as premier of the eastern region. Following sustained agitations by minority groups, a plebiscite was conducted, leading to the creation of a fourth, mid-west region, with Denis Osadebe as premier.

The central government under Tafawa Balewa put in place the requisite infrastructure for the good governance of the country. In 1962, the Balewa administration initiated the First National Development Plan for the infrastructure development of the new nation. Under the plan, the Balewa administration successfully implemented the development of the following infrastructure, among others:

- The niger dams authority in 1962
- The 1964 niger bridge in Onitsha, which linked the eastern and western parts of the country
- Bacita sugar mill in 1964
- Jebba paper mill in 1965
- The Oil refining company in Port-Harcout, 1965

The clear separation of power between the central government and the regional governments between 1960 and 1966, coupled with the political and economic autonomy the regions enjoyed, led to healthy competition in the development of infrastructure, with some positive results:

1 The western region, due to its government's free education policy, saw widespread development of educational infrastructure. More schools and access roads were constructed, with pipe-borne water servicing the schools. The Awolowo administration also built the University of Ife, the first-class infrastructure of which is comparable to that found in the developed world. In addition, the western regional government built the high-rise cocoa house in Ibadan, as a testament to the rich cash crop, and established the first television service in black Africa.
2 The northern regional government, for its part, established and built the Ahmadu Bello University in Zaria, to advance education in the region. They embarked on aggressive agricultural program, producing cash crops like cotton and groundnuts, culminating in the famous groundnut pyramids in Kano.
3 The eastern regional government established and built the University of Nigeria to "promote the dignity of man", as Nnamdi Azikiwe put it. The region also embraced agriculture, producing cash crops such as rubber and palm oil, and began developing their coal reserves to generate electricity.
4 The new mid-western region under Osadebe was busy establishing governance infrastructure while rapidly expanding its palm and rubber plantations. The Osadebe government also established a textile mill in Asaba. Cash crops like cocoa, palm oil, and rubber were produced in this region.

The prevalent equity and healthy competition saw each region develop at its own pace between the period 1958 and 1966. From 1960–1966, the political leaders were still learning the ropes and gradually adapting to the parliamentary system of government, faltering sometimes but rising as often as they fell. These leaders endured until the military overthrew the government in January 1966, setting aside the republican constitution of the young country and abrogating the parliamentary system. In its place, the military imposed a unitary system of government, in which political power was concentrated at the center, at the expense of the autonomy of the regions. The unitary system meant that the regional governments lost their autonomy and capacity to exercise control over mineral deposits in their regions and develop at their own pace. The mineral resources in the regions were now controlled by the central government, in line with military command and control, where power and authority flow from top to bottom. Thus began the central government's practice of appropriating resources in the regions into a common pool, from which they provided monthly allocations to the regional governments, with dire consequences for infrastructure development. The emergent unitary system neither motivated hard work nor fostered the type of healthy competition in infrastructure development that had been in place in the first republic.

During the long military era that followed, the government of Nigeria embarked on a desperate search for a political system that would work better for the nation. A drastic political reform began when the country embraced and adopted the presidential system of government, with a federal constitution fashioned after the American democratic system. This represented a significant political reform in Nigeria and ushered in the Shagari's presidential political leadership through a multi-party system of government (Ado-Kurawa, 2005).

The political process in Nigeria transitioned from the parliamentary system that had existed during the first republic to a presidential system in the second republic. The series of military interventions in the nation's political history made clear that its infrastructure problem had little or nothing to do with its political system. Rather, it had more to do with ineffective leadership; poor governance; and a host of other social issues, such as tribalism, corruption, religious intolerance, and lack of patriotism (Transparency International, 2010).

Under the political leadership of Yakubu Gowon (1966–1975), new states were created by military fiat during the Nigerian Civil War, often called the Biafran War. By the time the war ended in 1970, the country's geo-political map had changed from a four-regional structure to a country of 12 states, with the mid-western region remaining a single state.

State creation as a socio-political reform measure was based on the assumption that Nigerians would abandon regional and ethnic allegiances and embrace national unity. Based on this philosophy, its subsequent political leaderships, namely the Muhammed, Babangida, and Abacha administrations, created more states by military fiat, bringing the total number to 36 by the year 2010.

While state creation may have brought government activities closer to Nigerians and generated rural development, it also led to another type of social problem in Nigeria. Privileged Nigerians began to focus more on misappropriating state resources recklessly, often going unchallenged. With the creation of more states came the pressure to create more local government authorities. Nigeria has 744 local governments, serving as the third level of government. Although this was a significant political reform in Nigeria, many believe that tribalism and nepotism, rather than justice and fairness, informed the distribution of new states and local governments by the Babangida and Abacha administrations. This has led to the unabated call for balancing among the former eastern, western, and mid-western regions, who feel shortchanged, not only in the share of national revenue and projects, but also in political considerations, such as the demarcation of state and federal constituencies, due to lopsidedness in states and local governments creation.

The implication for infrastructure development is that, apart from the federal and state governments, where infrastructure for governance is expected to be put in place, the same had to be replicated in the 774 local government areas across the country. This led to more roads, schools, pipe-borne water, provision of electricity in rural areas, housing, and a host of other infrastructure.

The quest for political stability in Nigeria led to two attempts at reforming the constitution. A new constitution for the third republic was drafted, debated, and approved in 1989 during the Babangida administration, but was not proclaimed. In 1999, rather than proclaim the approved 1989 constitution, the military government set up a committee of 'handpicked' members to review the constitution written by the Abacha military government for his planned transmutation from a military dictator into a civilian president and recommend amendments that would encourage good governance. The undemocratic nature of this committee, and its deference to the military leaders, meant that the 1999 constitution couldn't be said to be the peoples' constitution.

In 2003, the national assembly set up a committee to review the 1999 constitution. In 2005, a national political reform conference was convened by Obasanjo's administration and charged with the responsibility of producing far-reaching constitutional changes. The report of the national political reform conference touched on several issues, including the political rights of minorities, the creation of states and local governments, the role of traditional institutions, the revenue allocation formula, and how to reform the electoral process.

The totality of the constitutional reform efforts by successive administrations in Nigeria resulted in the Electoral Act of 2006 and the nature and outcome of the 2007 elections. Again, in 2014, a national gathering of ethnic nationalities was held in Abuja and published a report that everyone thought would solve the country's socio-political problems. However, the report was neither proclaimed nor implemented.

An important aspect of the socio-political reform in Nigeria was in the measures taken by the political leaderships between 1960 and 2015 to improve the electoral process. At the core of the country's social and political unrest has been the constant problem of election rigging and results that claim to elect individuals who were never elected by the people. Songi (2008) and Ado-Kurawa (2005) pointed out that the electoral process in Nigeria has been anything but free and fair and can best be described as a mockery of democracy.

Elections in Nigeria have been characterized by violence, malpractices, and controversies (Ploch, 2010; Songi, 2008). As they pointed out, Nigerians have not had a voice or a choice in the electoral process, and the pervasive culture of impunity and executive lawlessness in governance have nourished and intensified competitive rigging. The independent national electoral commission (INEC) often had vested interest in the results of elections in Nigeria. Although the Electoral Act of 2006 made provisions for sanctions and punitive measures to be exerted on electoral offenders, no one has ever been successfully prosecuted and punished (Songi, 2008).

Despite the electoral problems in Nigeria, the reform process achieved some recognizable progress between 1960 and 2015. This includes limitation on political leaders' terms of office. Furthermore, the fact that for the first time in the Nigerian political history, a smooth transfer of government from a civilian administration to another civilian administration occurred in 2007. This was repeated in 2011, and more importantly, in 2015, for the first time, the ruling party ceded power to the main opposition party without rancor or bitterness. Since then, the legislative arm of government (the National Assembly) has been able to hold the executive arm of government accountable – a significant departure from common practices under draconian military regimes.

Economic reforms

At the country's independence in 1960, the Nigerian economy of the first republic was heavily based on agricultural production, which was mainly to satisfy domestic consumption needs, although some of the produce were exported. The second National Development Plan (1970–1974) focused on rural development and the growth of the agricultural sector. Rural roads were constructed to facilitate the transportation of agricultural produce to the markets and the seaports. It was during the military administration of Yakubu Gowon that the economic status of Nigeria took a boost with oil production and revenue generated from exporting petroleum products. The third National Development Plan (1975–1980) and the fourth National Development Plan (1981–1985) indicated a period of progressive economic prosperity, which brought about significant economic reforms. Key initiatives included privatization, energy reforms, poverty reduction, the National Economic Empowerment and Development Strategy (NEEDS) program, banking and insurance sector reform, and upgrade in telecommunications. At this stage, it will be helpful to review all of those.

Privatization

The privatization policy of the Federal Government of Nigeria was a significant economic reform that helped to redirect public sector governance. Between 1999 and 2006, about 116 enterprises were privatized in Nigeria, including various loss-making, government-owned enterprises operating in industries such as aluminum, telecommunications, petrochemical, insurance, and hospitality. Privatization of about 116 enterprises meant that new owners came on board, and fresh capital was injected for the proper functioning and expansion of these enterprises, which sometimes involved the development of new infrastructure to support production and distribution.

Nigerians took charge of most of the privatized enterprises and turned them around, achieving profitability while providing employment to citizens. A major component of the privatization program was the unbundling of the Power Holding Company of Nigeria (PHCN) into 18 companies responsible for power generation, transmission, and distribution.

Reform in the energy sector

Reform in the energy sector of the Nigerian economy has been gradual and steady. At its independence in 1960, the nation's main energy supply came from coal and the National Electric Power Authority (NEPA). Neither the supply of coal nor the electricity output was adequate, which made energy reforms imperative. Between the first republic and 2015, significant energy reforms were put in place, especially following the discovery of oil and liquefied natural gas (LNG) being in abundance in Nigeria.

The following phases of Nigerian energy reform can be identified:

- Government encouragement of the private sector to invest in the electricity industry, thereby breaking up NEPA's monopoly and generating competition.
- Establishment of the Nigerian Electricity Regulatory Commission (NERC) to supervise and regulate the energy policy of the government.
- Privatization of the energy industry to encourage competitiveness.
- Creation of consumer awareness on the efficient use of energy.
- Initiation of a deregulation program.

Poverty reduction

A major economic reform program in Nigeria was initiated during President Olusegun Obasanjo's administration (1999–2007). In 2000, the government launched a Poverty Alleviation Program (PAP); an emergency measure aimed at poverty reduction, creation of employment, construction of rural infrastructure to stimulate growth, and provision of amenities such as water and electricity. The PAP developed into a more elaborate economic reform package called the NEEDS.

The National Economic Empowerment and Development Strategy (NEEDS)

NEEDS was set up in 2003 in direct response to the crises the Nigerian economy was facing at the start of the millennium. The country was experiencing policy instability, rising poverty levels, poor governance, a high rate of inflation, unemployment, a huge budget deficit, corruption, and the near collapse of its social and economic infrastructure. It was against this background that NEEDS was introduced as an economic reform program. Its primary goal was to achieve poverty reduction, and its focus was on employment generation, wealth creation, and value reorientation. Its underlying strategy was to promote the private sector as the engine for growth. To ensure its success, the National Planning Commission (2007) identified the following critical imperatives:

- Promoting justice and good governance, in addition to promoting constitutional democracy, fighting corruption, and upholding the rule of the law.
- Ensuring security of life and property to attract domestic and foreign investments to boost economic growth.
- Pursuing an aggressive policy on the development of physical infrastructure as well as maintaining and rehabilitating existing infrastructure.
- Developing a professional and result-oriented public service that can transform the socio-economic framework of the nation.
- Strengthening the bonds of collaboration among all tiers of the federal system of government to promote good governance.

Some have argued that the NEEDS policy did not significantly differ from previous development plans by the government, despite claims to the contrary. Economic and policy experts pointed out that poor prioritization of policies and programs, and leadership's lack of commitment kept the country from achieving the objectives of the policy.

However, the aggressive development of physical infrastructural facilities positively impacted on infrastructure development in Nigeria. New roads were built, and existing roads in poor conditions were rehabilitated. Skills acquisition centers were established in various states and local government areas, and women and youth were trained, so they might be able to earn a living and improve their quality of life. New primary health centers were built in all 774 local government areas to improve the health of their citizens.

Banking and insurance sector reform

Another economic reform program in the period under review was the banking sector reform. Prior to this, the Nigerian banking sector was fragmented and under-capitalized due to its poorly managed liberalization during the structural adjustment program of the 1980s. To strengthen the financial sector and improve the availability of domestic credit to the private sector, a bank consolidation exercise was launched in 2004 that required commercial banks to raise their minimum capital base from $15 million to $192 million by the end of 2005. Some commercial banks merged because of this reform, bringing about financial solvency and economic stability.

The reform of the insurance sector consolidated about 100 insurance companies that existed in 2004 to about 30. This consolidation, along with a capitalization of about $1.6 billion, resulted in significant savings and brought significant economic prosperity to the sector.

Telecommunications reform

Telecommunications reform constitutes a significant economic reform program in Nigeria. At independence in 1960, telecommunication was in its infancy, with only a single telephone services company in operation. Different political administrations had taken measures to improve telecommunication in Nigeria. Its reform helped to open the market to local and foreign private investors, thereby injecting competition and improvement into this sector. The Nigerian Communications Commission (NCC) reported that an estimated US$37.5 billion was invested in the telecommunications sector between 2003 and 2007, resulting in ownership of telephones increasing from 450,000 in 1999 to 38 million in 2007, 85 million by 2010, and about 115 million by 2015. Government reform of the telecommunications sector was primarily enacted through deregulation, which eliminated monopolies. The reform process included:

- Privatization, which resulted in selling state-owned companies and establishing private operators.
- The introduction of the Mobile Telephony System in Nigeria in 1992.
- The introduction of the National Telecommunication Policy in 2000.

The benefits of the telecommunication reforms in Nigeria have been:

- Telecommunication services now being readily available to many Nigerians, including consumers in rural communities.
- General improvement in the quality of telecommunication services provided by companies.
- Lower service cost brought about by competition.
- Enhanced tele-density in the country.

Other financial reforms

Financial sector reforms in Nigeria included the policy of budgeting based on a conservative oil price benchmark, which resulted in the creation of an Excess Crude Account in 2003. This had the positive outcome of dedicated funds for infrastructure and economic development. The evolutionary stages of such financial reforms in the country had their roots in the pre-independence era in 1950 and were comprised of three phases:

1. The foundation phase between 1950 and 1970 was characterized by the establishment of financial institutions and the development of the necessary legal framework. During this phase, the Central Bank of Nigeria (CBN) was established.
2. The expansion phase between 1970 and 1985, during which commercial banks established branches in the rural and semi-urban areas, made lending to the private sector more accessible.
3. The consolidation and reform phase started in 1986 and continued to 2015 under different political leaderships in Nigeria. Prominent reforms of this phase included the initiation of the Structural Adjustment Program (SAP), which started in 1986, and the establishment of the Nigeria Deposit Insurance Corporation (NDIC) under the Babangida administration.

Although the structural adjustment program was aimed at economic growth and poverty reduction, the program led to an increase in the gap between the rich and the poor, and an intensification of poverty in Nigeria.

The trade policy reform was another important economic measure aimed at establishing good governance. Following the SAP in 1988, a seven-year tariff schedule that significantly reduced tariff averages was adopted leading to the introduction of policies on import prohibitions. These banned the import of selected products that were viewed as strategic for the growth of the economy in order to protect infant industries. By liberalizing its import regime and adopting the common external tariff (CET) of the Economic Community of West African States (ECOWAS), Nigeria's trade policies became more transparent and predictable, thereby enhancing good governance.

Administrative reforms: the civil service

The Nigerian civil service constitutes the administrative arm of the federal government of Nigeria. Political leaderships come and go, but the civil service remains to serve each government. Essentially, its role in public sector governance and infrastructure development cannot be overemphasized. The civil service is a body of government employees entrusted with the administration of the country and mandated to carry out the policies of government. Following independence, the country faced the challenge of replacing expatriate colonial administrators with well-trained Nigerian civil servants. Such a nationalization of the civil service was a daunting task. As a result of aggressive staff development programs, qualified Nigerians were able to take over and administer the civil service. During the military administrations, however, the civil service became politicized, and corruption became the norm of the day, threatening to engulf the civil servants as transparency and accountability were undermined. Consequently, the methods, standards, and scales of the civil service dropped, jeopardizing good governance. As a result, the civil service witnessed some decline. Some of the factors responsible for this included weak performance by ill-trained management staff; lack of proper manpower planning, and the removal of occupational classifications by the Udorji Commission in 1974. The 1988 reforms introduced by the Babangida administration recognized the politicization of the civil service and initiated major changes. Administrators were appointed by the political leadership, and promotions were no longer based on merit. The top civil servants became very powerful public officers with allegiance to politicians, rather than to the Nigerian nation. Successive governments took some measures to reform the Nigerian civil service, including:

- Demilitarization, which ensured that the system was guided by the constitutional provisions, the public service rules, and the financial regulations.
- Reintroduction of the pooling system, which ensured that all officers were assigned appropriate tasks that enhanced professionalism, harmonized development, and led to the efficient transfer of skills and talents within the service.
- Restoration of the office of the Head of Civil Service, which aimed at providing solid leadership, maintaining political neutrality, and improving staff welfare.
- Centralization of training for all categories of staff, which ensured efficient manpower development.
- Comprehensive restructuring of the civil service system, which helped to streamline roles and responsibilities, and define expectations.

Despite these reforms, major problems continued to exist in the Nigerian civil service. First, civil servants were poorly paid. The Udoji commission identified this as one of the reasons for the civil service mediocre performance, and a trigger for corruption, which eventually became endemic. Favoritism and the politicization of the civil service also constituted major stumbling blocks. A final issue was inadequate training, especially in technology. Openness and objectivity of the recruitment and selection process, as well as the strategic development of staff for optimal utilization, are known to be some of the steps that can lead to improvement in the

setbacks faced by the ATA, it is no secret that it led to major success and received widespread support from both national and international communities. However, the Jonathan administration was only in power for four years, and the succeeding administration did not continue with the ATA. As a result, its success was not given enough time to mature, and so, the full potential of the agenda and most of the reforms put in place were not realized.

Commercialization and privatization

The commercialization and privatization policy brought about expansion in industries and companies privatized by the government. And with that came the development of requisite infrastructure along the value-chain of these businesses in order to accommodate the increased capacities. For example, privatized and commercialized banks embarked on massive branch development, bringing banking services to previously unserved and under-served communities in both rural and urban areas.

For the infrastructure sector, the government created the Infrastructure Concession and Regulatory Commission (ICRC) to incubate and regulate public-private partnerships in the development and expansion of critical national infrastructure. This came from the realization that government alone could not fund such development in Nigeria. Major developments that have been completed and are ongoing include the Murtala Muhammed International Airport Terminal 2 building, the Lekki toll road in Lagos, the second Niger bridge in Onitsha, and the Bodo-Bonny highway (with three main bridges). Several other concessions have been recorded in Nigeria, such as telecommunications, the petrochemical and aluminum industries, insurance, and the hospitality business. Concession of seaports has led to the emergence of private port operators, who are investing in the provision of ports infrastructure.

The integrated approach to transportation

An integrated approach has led to the development of inter-modal transportation in Nigeria. Concerted efforts have been made to develop arterial roads, national rail lines, airports, and seaports in a way that promotes inter-modalism in transportation. However, more private sector participation is needed to raise the capital required for further development of the transportation sector.

Education policy

One of the challenges after independence was filling the many vacancies in the civil service with qualified Nigerians. This led to the formulation of education policies that placed an emphasis on Western education.

The subsequent commencement of universal free primary education by Obasanjo's military administration in 1976 further promoted this policy, which saw all Nigerians of school age attending primary school to receive a six-year basic education. Later policies of the civil democratic administration adopted the 6-3-3-4 policy, which increased the period of basic education to nine years (6-3). This has led to the education of many Nigerians, with those who can afford it furthering their education even more at colleges of education, polytechnics and universities. This education policy has led to a more skilled and qualified population in Nigeria. Consequently, Nigerians are now excelling in every profession in various parts of the world.

Good governance

Adherence to good governance is the differentiating factor that separates administrations that have succeeded in infrastructure development from those that have not. Good governance must be perceived to solve socio-economic and political problems and should be focused on the welfare of the people. Provision of infrastructure that promotes the economic well-being of citizens is one good indication of good governance. It promotes accountability and transparency in project selection and ensures the efficient management of resources in developing needed infrastructure that will serve as a catalyst for economic growth and well-being of citizens.

Macro-economic and financial reforms

The reforms that have had the greatest impact on the economy are the macro-economic reforms that led to its triple growth, from about 2% to 6%, resulting in a stable exchange rate, single digit inflation, narrow fiscal deficit, and good balance of payments (Okonjo-Iweala, 2012). The reforms on the macro side have also encouraged administrations to pay attention to what is wrong in the infrastructure sector and helped them to realize that the growth rate of the economy cannot be sustained without adequate investment in infrastructure.

Other reforms

- **The tenure policy,** which motivated the work force towards better service delivery.
- **The National Development Plans**, which ensured the development of infrastructure in an orderly manner with fiscal discipline.
- **Total Radar Coverage of Nigeria** (TRACON) policy.
- **Commercialization and privatization** policy.
- **Infrastructure development intervention agencies**, such as the Petroleum Trust Fund (PTF), which aimed at the rehabilitation of existing and ailing infrastructure nationwide.

- **Niger Delta Development Commission**, mandated to develop infrastructure in the oil-rich region.
- **The Procurement Reform**, which created and enhanced transparency in government tenders and projects.

Summary

This chapter set out to answer the following question: how did the various reforms of the different political eras affect the development of infrastructure in Nigeria between 1960 and 2015? To answer the question, we examined the socio-political, economic, and administrative reforms under its various leaders. The factors that contributed to the success of the reforms were reviewed; these included rural development, agricultural transformation, commercialization and privatization, transportation, education, and good governance.

Bibliography

Ado-Kurawa, G. (2005). *Nigerian politics and national political reforms.* Conference Paper. Lagos: Tellettes Publishing House.

Afeikhena, J. (2002). *Public enterprises reform in Nigeria: Evidence from the telecommunications industry.* Nairobi: African Economic Research Consortium.

Africa, G. (2014). *Fertilizer subsidy reform revives Nigeria's agriculture: Case studies on public-private agriculture investments.* Retrieved from www.growafrica.com

Anigbogu, N. A., & Shwarka, M. S. (2011). Evaluation of the impact of the public procurement reform program on combating corrupt practices in public building projects delivery in Nigeria. *Environtech Journal, 1*(2), 43–51. Retrieved from www.google.com

Ekpenkhio, S. A. (2003). *Public sector procurement reforms: The Nigerian experience.* Conference Paper. Nigeria. Retrieved from www.wto.org

Ezeh, E. M. (2013). *Public procurement reform strategies.* Retrieved from https://cips.org/Documents/Engr.%20Emeka%20Ezeh%20presentation%20%2821%20May%29%20%5BRepaired%5D.pdf

Jonathan, G. (2015). *Innovative reforms of President Goodluck Jonathan's administration* (pp. 17–24). Abuja: The Office of the Chief Economic Adviser to the President.

Marcellus, I. C. (2009). Development planning in Nigeria: Reflections on the national economic empowerment and development strategies (NEEDS) 2003–2007. *Journal of Social Sciences, 20*(30), 197–210.

Mbanefo, C. A. (2000). The role of engineering infrastructure in national development. In M. D. Abdullahi (Ed.), *Provision & maintenance of engineering infrastructure for technological development in Nigeria* (pp. 37–44). Kaduna: Fahimta Publishing Company.

Mohammed, K., Chapola, D., & Bello, A. (2013). The state of Nigerian economy in the 21st century: Privatization and commercialization programs under Obasanjo-Atiku regime. *European Scientific Journal, 9*(19), 88–98. Retrieved from http://eujournal.org/index.php/esj/

National Planning Commission. (2007). National report. The presidency, federal republic of Nigeria.

Naswem, A. A., Okwoche, V. A., & Age, A. I. (2016). Mainstreaming sustainability in the Nigerian agricultural transformation agenda. *World, 3*(1), 054–059.

Natsa, R. (2015). *Nigeria: As FG launches ATA-SP Phase 1*. All Africa. Retrieved from http://allafrica.com/stories/201503130138.html

Nzongola-Ntalaja, G. (2002). UNDP role in promoting good governance. Seminar for the International Guest at the Congress of the Labor Party, Oslo, Norway. Retrieved from www.um.edu.mt/_data/assets/pdf_file/0003/120837/2009_4.pdf

Ogbonna, B. C. (2012). Structural adjustment program (SAP) in Nigeria. An empirical assessment. *Journal of Banking, 6*(1), 19–40. Retrieved from www.academia.edu/

Ogbonna, A. C. & Kalu, L. U. (2012). Public procurement reform in developing countries: A critique of the real estate context in the Nigerian case. *International Journal of Management Sciences and Business Research, 1*(8), 65–77. Retrieved from www.ijmsbr.com/

Ogujiuba, K., & Obiechina, M. E. (2011). Financial sector reforms in Nigeria: Issues and challenges. *International Journal of Business and Management, 6*(6), 222–233. doi:10.5539/ijbm.v6n6p222

Okonjo-Iweala, N. (2012). *Reforming the unreformable: Lessons from Nigeria*. Cambridge, MA: The MIT Press.

Okonjo-Iweala, N., & Osafo-Kwaako, P. (2007). *Nigeria's economic reforms: Progress and challenges*. Retrieved from www.brokings.edu/research/papers/200

Olaopa, T. (2010). *Public service reforms in Africa*. Ibadan: University Press Plc.

Olumide, H. A. (2011). Telecommunication reform and effects of competition on availability, quality and cost of services in Nigeria. *Public Policy and Administration Research, 1*(3), 8–20. Retrieved from www.iist.org/Journals/index.php/PPAR

Ploch, L. (2010). Nigeria: CRS report for congress. *Congressional Research Service,* 7(5700), 1–35. Retrieved from www.crs.gov

Songi, O. (2008). *Electoral reform in Nigeria: Prospects and challenges*. Retrieved from http//works.bepress.com

Taye, O. O., & Dada, M. O. (2012). Appraisal of private sector involvement in infrastructure development in Lagos, Nigeria. *Mediterranean Journal of Social Sciences, 3*(2), 399–412. doi:10.5901/mjss.2012.v3n2.399

Therkildsen, O. (2001). Efficiency, accountability and implementation: Public sector reforms in East and Southern Africa. Democracy, Governance and Human Rights; UNRISD. Retrieved from www.unrisd.org

Transparency International. (2010). Corruption perceptions index. Retrieved from www.transparency.org/cpi2010/results

Udoka, C. A., & Anyingang, R. A. (2012). The effects of privatization on economic growth on Nigeria: 1979–2007 in retrospect. *International Journal of Economic Development, Research and Investment, 3*(2), 25–35. Retrieved from www.icidr.org/

UNDP. (1997). Reconceptualizing governance. Discussion paper 2, Management Development and Governance.

5 The national development plans

Origins of planning for development in Nigeria

The origins of planning for development in Nigeria can be traced back to 1946, when the British colonial administration introduced a "ten-year plan of development and welfare for Nigeria" using the colonial development and welfare fund. Under this plan, N110 million was earmarked, mostly for building a transport and communication system for the colony in order to facilitate the transportation of various agricultural produce to the seaports for export to meet the needs of manufacturing industries in England. According to Akinwale (2010), based on this foundational plan, the colonial administrators were able to provide tarred roads of minimal dimensions as well as railways, ports, urban electricity, health centers, schools, basic communication networks, and a few other infrastructures that supported colonial governance in Nigeria.

The national development plans were conceived with the intent of improving on the minimal infrastructure inherited from the pre-independence colonial administration and transforming the newly independent nation from a traditional society into a modern society, where political independence would lead to macroeconomic stability, viable domestic and international trade, infrastructure development, industrialization, employment of citizens in productive engagements, and economic prosperity for the country and its people.

First National Development Plan (1962–1968)

Following the attainment of political independence from Britain on October 1, 1960, the Balewa government began to prepare the First National Development Plan for the federal and regional governments. The plan was launched in April 1962 with the objective of maintaining an average growth rate of 4% of its gross domestic product at constant prices. To achieve this, the government planned to invest about 15% of the country's gross national domestic product each year and ensure that this gross fixed investment was channeled into the productive sector of the economy. The government hoped that this initiative would serve as a catalyst for economic growth and development, and bring about prosperity for the new nation.

Goals for the First National Development Plan:

- Equitable distribution of national income
- A ramp-up of the economic growth rate
- Generation of investments to reduce dependence on foreign capital for the development of the nation
- Enough capital for the development of manpower
- Increased standard of living for citizens, particularly with respect to food, housing, health, and clothing
- Development of infrastructure

Under the First National Development Plan, a total investment expenditure of N2.13 billion was proposed. This consisted of public sector investment of N1.35 billion, with the balance of N780 million expected to come from the private sector.

The federal capital expenditure program (see Table 5.1) reflected the aims of the National development plan. The federal government allocated almost 70% to economic development expenditure as opposed to the 55% it had offered in the previous plan. The 15% improvement in economic development expenditure reflected the hunger for rapid development in Nigeria by the post-colonial Balewa administration. The regional governments maintained this trend. In the western region, the 1962–1968 national development plan projected expenditure in agriculture and industry at more than 40% of total capital expenditure, as compared with the approximately 20% of public capital earmarked for investment in these sectors since 1955. In the northern region, the shift was from 15% to more than 30%. These trends portrayed the first republic government as one that was poised to bring about economic growth and development in Nigeria.

The full implementation of the first national development plan was interrupted by two major events: the military coup in 1966 and the civil war of 1967, which lasted for three years. As such, the plan was extended to 1970. Nevertheless, the federal government and regional governments recorded key achievements during the implementation period of the first National Development Plan before the military intervention of 1966.

The post-independence Balewa government successfully implemented many strategic projects, including:

a A sugar mill in Bacita,
b A paper mill in Jebba,
c The niger dam in Kainji,
d The niger bridge in Onitsha,
e An oil refinery in Port Harcout,
f Seaport extension in Lagos
g Some "trunk A" roads across Nigeria.

Table 5.1 Showing federal capital expenditure program, 1962–1968

Distribution by sector in millions		*1955 – 1961 Program*		*1962 – 1968 Program*	
		Actual expenditure 1955 – 1961	%	*Actual expenditure 1962 – 1968*	%
I. Economic					
1	Primary Production	1.2	0.8	20.5	5
2	Trade and Industry	3.8	2.6	44	10.7
3	Electricity	7	4.8	98.1	23.8
4	Transport	49.9	34	104	25.1
5	Communications	12.1	8.3	30	7.3
6	Water excl. irrigation	2	2	1.8	0.4
II. Social overhead					
7	Education	6.8	4.6	29.2	7.1
8	Health	2.9	2	10.3	2.5
9	Town and Country Planning	17.4	11.9	23.2	5.6
10	Social Welfare	0.4	0.3	2.7	0.7
11	Information	1	0.7	2.3	0.6
III. General administration					
12	Judicial	0.1	0.1	0.3	0.1
13	General	35.7	24.4	43.9	10.6
IV. Financial obligations					
14	Financial Obligations	6.1	4.1	2.2	0.5
	Total	146.3	100	412.5	100
I.	Development	76	51.9	298.4	72.3
II.	Social Overhead	28.4	19.5	67.7	16.5
III.	General Administration	35.7	24.4	44.2	10.7
IV.	Financial Obligations	6.1	4.1	2.2	0.5
	Total	146.3	100	412.5	100

Source: Federal government development program 1962–1968 (Sessional Paper No. 1 of 1962). Federal Printing Division, Lagos.

The first generation of Nigerian universities were also built: the University of Ibadan and University of Lagos, established by the federal government; Ahmadu Bello University, Zaria, established by the northern Nigeria regional government; the University of Nigeria, Nsukka, established by the eastern Nigeria regional government; and the University of Ife, established by the western Nigeria regional government.

Table 5.2 Distribution of capital programs among expenditure categories (all governments) 1955–1961 and 1962–1968

	1955–1961 Plan (%)	*1962–1968 Plan (%)*
Development expenditure	50.80%	71.70%
Social overhead expenditure	19.90%	20.90%
Administrative expenditure	29.30%	7.00%

Source: Federal government development program 1962–1968 (Sessional Paper No. 1 of 1962). Federal Printing Division, Lagos.

It is noteworthy that the federal and regional governments could accomplish these laudable projects despite the challenges of governance at the time. The successes recorded could be attributed to the fidelity to the annual budgets and the national development plan framework, thus removing arbitrariness from budgeting and project selection. The development plan provided guidelines for meaningful and coordinated development during the plan period. There was also discipline, resulting in the devotion of about 72% of the budget to capital expenditure, 21% to socials, and 7% to overheads.

In order to attain the growth objectives stated in the plan, there had to be a substantial shift in the composition of capital expenditure to directly productive investments in the 1962–1968 program, as compared with the 1955–1961 program. For instance, investment in industry, agriculture, and mining, which generated income at a higher and faster rate, was accorded a greater percentage than administration, usually considered an area of "low" pay-offs on investment. Table 5.2 compares the public investment pattern of the 1962–1968 plan with that of the preceding colonial administration.

Second National Development Plan (1970–1975)

Shortly after the end of the civil war in 1970, Yakubu Gowon, then military head of state, launched the Second National Development Plan for the federal government and the 12 states of the federation, covering the five-year period 1970–1975. As a post-war development plan, it focused on reconstruction of the economy, rehabilitation, and reintegration. The Second National Development Plan had as its objectives:

- The building of a united, strong, and self-reliant nation
- A great and dynamic economy
- A just and egalitarian society
- A land of bright and full opportunities for all its citizens
- A free and democratic society

Part of the strategy adopted by the federal government to achieve this was indigenization policy, which set a long-term objective of economic independence. This policy motivated Nigerians to participate fully in the commercial, industrial, and financial activities of the nation's economy.

The Second National Development Plan had a projected expenditure of N4.9 billion. While the public sector was expected to invest about N3.3 billion, the private sector was expected to make investments totaling about N1.6 billion. The federal government prioritized sectors such as transport, communication, manufacturing, housing, and education in the development plan. Although high priorities were given to agriculture and industry, this was not reflected in the plan's implementation. In the same vein, the objective to create a free and democratic society was not realized as the military hung on to power and trampled on citizens' rights. Worse still, the indigenization policy recorded only about 30% success. About 16 multinational companies representing American, Dutch, Japanese, British, Italian, German, and French interests kept their firm grip on the nation's oil and gas assets.

Despite these inadequacies, some successes were recorded in agriculture and industry. Many industries affected by the civil war were rehabilitated. For example, two salt factories were established in Kaduna. A super-phosphates project and two vehicle assembly plants were also built. Additional achievements under the second National Development Plan included the establishment of colleges of technology and trade centers by state governments, and construction of about 3,000 km of arterial roads and bridges across the country as well as the successful launch of the National Youth Service Corps (NYSC) scheme, aimed at achieving national integration, and the introduction of federal scholarships and loan schemes for Nigerian students.

Third National Development Plan (1975–1980)

In April 1975, the Third National Development Plan was launched by Yakubu Gowon, who had been the Nigerian military head of state since 1966, to cover the period 1975–1980. The plan's goal was to lay a solid foundation for Nigeria as:

- A united, strong, and self-reliant nation
- A strong and dynamic economy
- A just and egalitarian society
- A land full of opportunities for its citizens
- A free and democratic society

To realize these goals, specific, short-term objectives were articulated in the plan, including equitable distribution of income; reduction in unemployment; increase in the supply of high-level manpower; increase in per capital income; balanced development; and indigenization of economic activities. The strategy of the plan was to use resources from oil to develop the productive capacity of the economy and improve the standard of living of the citizenry. The plan was predicated on the public sector providing social facilities, such as urban housing, education, electricity and water supply, and health services for the poorer section of the population to improve the standard of living of the people.

The plan had a huge initial capital investment of N30 billion. The public sector was expected to contribute N20 billion of this amount, and the private sector contribution was pegged at N10 billion. In comparison to the first and second National Development Plans, the third plan was more ambitious as it proposed a growth rate of 9% against the proposed growth rates of 4% and 6.6%, respectively, of the first and second plans.

The implementation of the plan was hampered three months after its launch, when Murtala Mohammed assumed leadership via palace coup in July 1975. Specifically, the change of government resulted in a reappraisal of some of the objectives and strategies contained in the plan. Emphasis was placed on projects that had a direct effect on average citizens. However, a further change of government occurred through a bloody coup that saw the assassination of Mohammed. The people behind the coup, themselves, were overpowered by government forces, which led to the emergence of Olusegun Obasanjo as the military head of state in February 1976. This resulted in further reappraisal of the plan, with emphasis shifting to agriculture and manufacturing.

Assessment of the impact of the plan revealed that it failed to give priority to projects and programs that had direct impact on rural dwellers. An example of the sectoral misalignment between the plan and capital resource allocation is visible in agriculture and social development (i.e., housing, education, water supply, and health services), which directly affect the living conditions of the rural population. Only 5% and 11.5%, respectively, were allocated to these critical priority areas. The plan exacerbated rural-urban migration, leading to problems of overpopulation and unemployment in the urban areas, while the rural areas experienced a progressive decimation of their active workforce (ages 15–45), leaving only the very young and old behind.

One of the consequences of the migration pattern induced by the third National Development Plan was that only very few able farm workers were present to partake in agriculture, which had been the mainstay of the Nigerian economy before the discovery and exploitation of the newfound oil reserves, leading to a decline in agricultural outputs. The plan should have aimed to establish agro-processing industries in the rural areas as part of a concerted rural development plan, taking industries to the people and improving rural infrastructure and the economic well-being of rural dwellers. Instead, rural dwellers hitherto engaged in agriculture were lured to the urban areas to seek better jobs, and consequently swell unemployment levels. Nevertheless, the story was different for the manufacturing sector, which recorded a high growth rate of 18.1%. Other sectors that witnessed growth were building and construction.

However, rather than build on the regulatory framework contained in the second plan, the third plan seemed to have deliberately dismantled the controls that had been used in the past. As such, the ports were thrown open, and foreign exchange restrictions were relaxed. Private sector engagements in commerce, industry, agriculture, construction, and road transportation were subjected to little or no control. This led to Nigeria's economic woes. Within a year, the value of imports rose by more than 100%; miscellaneous manufactured goods recorded an increase of 102%; importation of machinery and equipment increased by 155%; food imports increased by 92%; and imports of beverages increased by a whopping 433%, turning Nigeria into a "dumping ground". A major effect of all these imports was that Nigeria's trade balance which stood at a surplus of N2.7 billion in 1974/1975, turned into a deficit of N125 million.

Fourth National Development Plan (1981–1985)

The Fourth National Development Plan was launched by President Shehu Shagari in 1981 on behalf of the federal government and the governments of the then 19 states of the federation to cover the period 1981–1985. It was the first plan to be prepared by a democratically elected government since the military intervention in Nigerian politics in 1966 and was under a new constitution based on the presidential system of government. The objectives of the plan were to achieve:

- An increase in the real income of the average citizen
- More even distribution of income among individuals and socio-economic groups
- Reduction in the level of unemployment and under-employment
- An increase in the supply of key manpower
- A reduction in the dependence of the economy on a narrow range of activities
- Increased participation of citizens in the ownership and management of productive enterprises
- Greater self-reliance; through increased dependence on local resources in seeking to achieve the various objectives of society
- Development of technology
- Increased productivity
- Promotion of a new national orientation conducive to greater discipline, better attitudes towards work, and a cleaner environment

The plan adopted as its main strategy the use of resources generated from oil to ensure uniform expansion in the production capacity of the economy and lay a foundation for self-sustaining growth. The fourth national development plan was the most ambitious plan yet, launched by the government of Nigeria. However, it too was affected by a change of government when Muhammadu Buhari overthrew the democratically elected government of President Shagari (after he had won a second term) in 1983.

The Buhari regime jettisoned the fourth National Development Plan and instead ruled by military decrees in a draconian style. Another military change of government in 1985, which brought in Ibrahim Babangida as head of state, further exacerbated the situation by adversely affecting the implementation of the plan's programs.

The development plan had a total capital investment of N82 billion, out of which the public sector was expected to invest about N70 billion, and the private sector's contribution was estimated to reach N12 billion. However, by 1984, only 54% of the export proceeds projected for the period were realized. And with limited resources to finance the plan, the economy witnessed debt service and balance of payment problems, coupled with inflation. Most of the projects that had been started at the introduction of the plan were abandoned.

The growth rate of Gross Domestic Product (GDP) per annum nosedived to about 1.25%. The consequential rise of the cost of living led to a reduction in the standard of living of the citizenry. There was a marked increase in unemployment during the period, and the country's foreign reserves maintained a steady decline. The plan period of 1981–1985 proved to be the worst in the economic history of Nigeria up to that time.

Despite the abysmal performance of the economy during this period, the fourth National Development Plan recorded some successes. These included the successful implementation of the Agricultural Development Program (ADP) in most states and the Dry Dock Project at Snake Island, Lagos. The introduction of 87 telephone exchanges located in various parts of the country led to an increase in the number of fixed telephone lines from 188,000 in 1981 to 297,000 by 1985.

It is worth stating that between 1985 and 1986, the concept of development planning was still common in Nigeria. However, after the end of this period, this concept gradually faded away, and a new planning paradigm emerged in Nigeria.

Fifth National Development Plan (1986–1990)

The Fifth National Development Plan was conceived due to the poor implementation of the fourth National Development Plan. Prior to the preparation of the plan, in November 1984, a conference was held at the University of Ibadan to deliberate on the appropriate mechanisms for the Fifth National Development Plan. The conference suggested some measures that served as a framework for the plan. Its objectives were:

- Diversification of the nation's economy from the prevalent monocultural (oil) economy
- Revitalization of the agricultural sector to achieve integrated rural development
- Domestic production of raw materials for local industries to reduce the importation of locally manufactured goods
- Promotion of employment opportunities to arrest the deterioration of unemployment

The plan focused on correcting structural defects in the economy and creating a more self-reliant version that would be regulated by market forces. The economy would be restructured in favor of the productive sector, especially the agriculture and manufacturing sectors that had been emphasized in the plan.

However, the Fifth National Development Plan did not materialize. The strategies were incorporated into the Structural Adjustment Program (SAP) introduced by the Babangida administration after the Nigerian public refused the recommendations of the International Monetary Fund (IMF), which entailed the devaluation of the economy and other austerity measures. The two-year SAP ended the five-year national development planning model in Nigeria. The two-year SAP model was again changed by the federal government to three-year rolling plans.

The perspective plan and rolling plans

The military administration under the leadership of Ibrahim Babangida abandoned the five-year development planning model and introduced the perspective plan, covering a period of 15–20 years. The intention was to focus on the long-term view of economic and development challenges facing the country. It established a rolling plan for a three-year period, with annual reviews to ensure that things were progressing according to the perspective plan and on track to meet long-term objectives.

While the rolling plans took off in 1990, the perspective plan from which they were to be derived did not take off until six years later, when the then military head of state, Sani Abacha, set up the vision 2010 committee. Although the committee submitted a final report on vision 2010, this was never launched by the federal government. Thus, for over ten years, no significant effort was made to embark on long-term planning for economic and infrastructure development. The rolling plan reinforced command and control leadership by the military, who succeeded in foisting a unitary system of government on Nigeria as the states lost autonomy, abandoned planning, and looked up to directives from the military-led government at the center.

Despite the abandonment of development planning, and its replacement with the three-year rolling plan by the Babangida administration (which steered the plans for nine years), some remarkable success in infrastructure development was recorded. Some of the accomplishments included:

- The construction of the 12 km Third Mainland Bridge, which was the longest bridge in Africa for about two decades.
- The construction of major trunk roads in the country
- Massive development of infrastructure in the new capital city, Abuja, which facilitated the relocation of the federal government from Lagos to Abuja
- The Minna township development plan and the launch of its implementation

- The Commencement of the Itakpe-Ajaokuta railway line
- The commencement of the Ajaokuta-Warri railway line (providing access to the seaport from the steel plant)
- The construction of an aluminum smelter plant in Ikot Abasi
- The completion of the federal secretariat, Abuja
- The construction of the Abuja International Conference Center
- The construction of Abuja International Airport
- The implementation of a privatization and commercialization policy

The Babangida administration also introduced programs that targeted the poorest members of society with a view to bringing them out of poverty. Examples include the establishment of the directorate of food, roads and rural infrastructure (DFRRI); the better life for rural women's program; and the people's bank, which gave loans to women and small and medium enterprises to boost their businesses and enhance their capacity to make a good living.

National economic empowerment and development strategy

Following the return to civil democratic governance in 1999, with the election of President Obasanjo under the platform of the People's Democratic Party (PDP), there was an urgent need to salvage the adverse economic situation resulting from years of military leadership. The negative effects included debilitating inflation, decaying infrastructure, a depressed civil service, rampant corruption, battered international image, and a largely disenchanted populace.

The Obasanjo government launched a poverty alleviation program (PAP) in 2000. This was an emergency measure aimed at poverty reduction, creation of employment, construction of rural infrastructure to stimulate growth, and provision of amenities such as water and electricity. By 2003, following the re-election of president Obasanjo, the PAP developed into a more elaborate economic reform package called the national economic empowerment and development strategy (NEEDS).

The NEEDS document was a roadmap to address the development challenges in Nigeria, having as its objectives the empowerment of citizens, wealth creation, employment generation, and poverty reduction. The NEEDS policy was expected to address the strain on the economy at the time, which was characterized by policy instability, rising poverty level, poor governance, high rate of inflation, unemployment, a huge budget deficit, corruption, and the near collapse of the social and economic infrastructure.

During this period, Nigeria's annual budgets rose to trillions of naira, yet the per capita income crashed to the level of the poorest countries in the world at one dollar per head. Phenomenal increase was recorded in the number of educational institutions.

Assessments of the NEEDS policy show that it was not different from the government's previous development plans. Ultimately, the policy as a development planning document did not achieve as many results as earlier national development plans. In terms of employment generation, for example, the policy set out to create about seven million jobs by 2007, but most of the policies adopted by the government to realize this goal were incompatible with job creation. In efforts to reform institutions of government, many employees lost their jobs, pointing to non-alignment between policies and objectives. Poor prioritization of policies and programs, and lack of good governance prevented the country from achieving the objectives of the policy.

Despite these shortcomings, the eight years of the Obasanjo administration resulted in a successful reduction of Nigeria's debt profile with the Bretton Wood Institutions, a combination of the World Bank and the IMF. Under Obasanjo, there were extensive efforts to revive and improve the country's telecommunication networks, increasing ownership of telephone lines in Nigeria from 450,000 in 1999 to 38 million in 2007. By 2010, the number was further ramped up to 85 million, and climbed to 115 million in 2015. The government also successfully privatized and commercialized many state-owned enterprises and established specialized institutions to tackle corruption and corrupt practices; the Economic and Financial Crimes Commission (EFCC) and the Independent Corrupt Practices Commission (ICPC). Obasanjo administration curbed inflation, increased the national minimum wage, improved Nigeria's poor international image occasioned by draconian military regimes of the past, and engineered Nigeria's first civilian-to-civilian transition to power, among other achievements.

Summary

The purpose of this chapter was to review the National Development Plans that guided policy and activities between 1962 and 1985. The first National Development Plan (1962–1968), the second National Development Plan (1970–1975), the third National Development Plan (1975–1980), and the fourth National Development Plan (1981–1985), all had sets of objectives and saw varying degrees of success. In 1984, toward the end of the fourth plan, discussions began on the preparation of a fifth national development plan. However, it never came into being. Instead, the leadership moved towards rolling plans for Nigeria, with a focus on more long-term planning to carry the country into the twenty-first century and a determination to pursue the 20:2020 vision that we will discuss in the next chapter.

Bibliography

Akinwale, A. A. (2010). The menace of inadequate infrastructure in Nigeria. *African Journal of Science, Technology, Innovation and Development*, 2(3), 207–228. Retrieved from www.ajstid.com

Lawal, T., & Oluwatoyin, A. (2011). National development in Nigeria: Issues, challenges and prospects. *Journal of Public Administration and Policy Research, 3*(9), 237–241. Retrieved from www.academicjournals.org

Marcellus, I. C. (2009). Development planning in Nigeria: Reflections on the national economic empowerment and development strategies (NEEDS) 2003–2007. *Journal of Social Sciences, 20*(30), 197–210.

Mbanefo, C. A. (2000). The role of engineering infrastructure in national development. In M. D. Abdullahi (Ed.), *Provision & maintenance of engineering infrastructure for technological development in Nigeria* (pp. 37–44). Kaduna: Fahimta Publishing Company.

National Planning Commission. (2007). National report. The presidency, federal republic of Nigeria.

National Planning Commission. (2009). Nigeria Vision 20:2020 economic transformation blueprint. The presidency, federal republic of Nigeria.

National Planning Commission. (2015). National integrated infrastructure master plan. The presidency, federal republic of Nigeria.

Naswem, A. A., Okwoche, V. A., & Age, A. I. (2016). Mainstreaming sustainability in the Nigerian agricultural transformation agenda. *World,* 3(1), 54–59.

Natsa, R. (2015). *Nigeria: As FG launches ATA-SP Phase 1.* All Africa. Retrieved from http://allafrica.com/stories/201503130138.html

Nwanolue, B. O. G., & Iwuoha, V. C. (2012). The Nigerian civil service and promotion of sustainable human development: A critical analysis. *Arabian Journal of Business and Management Review, 1*(9), 12–21. Retrieved from www.arabianjbmr.com

Obadan, M. I. (2003). *National development planning and budgeting in Nigeria: Some pertinent issues.* Lagos: Broadway Press Limited.

Olaseni, M., & Alade, W. (2012). Vision 20:2020 and the challenges of infrastructure development in Nigeria. *Journal of Sustainable Development, 5*(2), 1–14. doi:10.5539/jsd.v5n2p63

Taye, O. O., & Dada, M. O. (2012). Appraisal of private sector involvement in infrastructure development in Lagos, Nigeria. *Mediterranean Journal of Social Sciences, 3*(2), 399–412. doi:10.5901/mjss.2012.v3n2.399

Zuofa, T., & Ochieng, E. G. (2014). Project failure: The way forward and panacea for development. *International Journal of Business and Management, 9*(11), 59–71. Retrieved from www.ccsenet.org/ijbm

6 Vision 20:2020

The vision 20:2020 national development policy was launched by the Obasanjo administration (1999–2007). It was designed as a ten-year plan to stimulate Nigeria's economy and launch the country onto a path of rapid and sustained growth. The goal was to become one of the top 20 economies in the world, with a minimum GDP of 900 billion dollars by 2020.

The policy was based on a dynamic comparative analysis of the country's potential growth rate and economic structure vis-à-vis those of 40 other economies in the world. The assumption was that the Nigerian economy would grow at an average of 13.8% during the ten-year period, driven by the agricultural and industrial sectors.

Critical to the attainment of the vision were two broad objectives: the optimization of human and natural resources toward the attainment of rapid economic growth, and the translation of the resultant growth into equitable social development for all citizens. The roadmap for the realization of the vision included:

a Creating the platform for success by urgently addressing the most debilitating constraints to Nigeria's growth and competitiveness.

b Forging ahead with diligence and focus to develop the fabric of the envisioned economy by:

  i Aggressively pursuing a structural transformation from a mono-product economy to a diversified and industrialized economy.

  ii Investing to transform the Nigerian people into catalysts for growth and national renewal, and a lasting source of comparative advantage.

  iii Investing to create an environment that enables the coexistence of growth and development on an enduring and sustainable basis.

c Developing and deepening the capability of government to consistently translate national strategic intents into actions and results by instituting evidence-based decision making in Nigeria's public policy space.

As seen in Table 6.1, three pillars were identified in the vision 20:2020 policy as the building blocks of the desired future for Nigerians. The first pillar is the guarantee of the productivity and well-being of the citizens, leveraging on a population of 185 million, which represents one of the largest markets in the developing world. The second is the optimization of the key

Table 6.1 The three pillars of Vision 20:2020

	The pillars	*Strategic objectives*
The Vision: A large, strong, diversified, sustainable, and competitive economy that effectively harnesses the talents and energies of the people, and responsibly exploits its natural endowments to guarantee a high standard of living and quality of life to its citizens	Guaranteeing the productivity and well-being of the people	• Eradicate extreme hunger and poverty • Enhance access to quality and affordable health care • Provide accessible and affordable housing • Build human capacity for sustainable livelihoods and national development • Promote gender equality and empower women • Improve access to micro-credit • Foster a culture of entertainment and recreation for enhanced productivity
	Optimizing the key sources of economic growth	• Stimulate primary production to enhance the competitiveness of Nigeria's real sector • Significantly increase production of processed and manufactured goods for export • Stimulate domestic and foreign trade in value-adding goods and services • Strengthen linkages between key sectors of the economy
	Fostering sustainable social and economic development	• Develop efficient, accountable, transparent, and participatory governance • Establish a competitive business environment characterized by sustained macro-economic stability • Enhance national security and improve the administration of justice • Promote unity in diversity, national pride, and the conservation of the nation's cultural heritage • Develop sufficient and efficient infrastructure to support sustained economic growth • Preserve the environment for sustainable socio-economic development • Promote the sustainable development of Nigeria's geo-political regions into economic growth poles

sources of economic growth, which, in the Nigerian situation, is the rapid industrialization of the country's economy. The third pillar is fostering sustainable social and economic development. To achieve this, the government planned to enact the policy through three medium-term plans:

- First National Implementation Plan (2010–2013)
- Second National Implementation Plan (2014–2017)
- Third National Implementation Plan (2018–2020)

The implementation plans were expected to detail specific goals, strategies, and performance targets for all sectors of the economy and aligned with the overall strategy and principles of vision 20:2020. Institutionalizing monitoring and evaluation (M&E) across all levels of government was considered in the vision document to be the second critical lever in the implementation of this plan. An integrated M&E system was planned for this purpose. Executive-level demand for M&E information was to be generated through legislative action to mandate the annual presentation of the national performance report by the president to a joint session of the national assembly in a live broadcast on national television and radio to citizens of the country. This was to ensure political neutrality and accountability in the implementation of the policy. The envisaged vision 20:2020 legislation and the proposed project implementation continuity "Act" was intended to compel all tiers of government in Nigeria to create a multi-year development plan and implement the identified programs and projects.

The transformation agenda

To operationalize the first national implementation plan of vision 20:2020, a transformation agenda document was developed as a medium-term implementation framework. The document was developed to mitigate the age-long characteristics of Nigeria's developmental efforts: lack of continuity, consistency, and commitment to agreed policies, programs, and projects. It was expected that the transformation agenda would culminate in sustainable economic growth and development, with corresponding improvement in the overall welfare of Nigerian citizens. The document in its preamble adopted an unambiguous concept of infrastructure to be funded under the medium-term framework. The first national implementation plan, as articulated in the transformation agenda document, could not commence in 2010 as envisaged but was launched in 2012 with a focus on conceptualizing infrastructure.

Conceptualizing infrastructure

According to Craven (2012), infrastructure refers to a broad spectrum of facilities that derive from engineering activities for the use and convenience of people, such as transport (road, rail, water, and air), water

Table 6.2 The concept and scope of infrastructure under the first NIP

	In scope (examples)	Out of scope (examples)
Transport	Road, rail, port, and airport: include investment in building the asset (e.g. construction equipment cost)	Asset usage equipment (e.g. buses, cars, railway wagons, aircrafts, water ships)
Energy	Generation, transmission, and distribution (includes power equipment like BTG) Refineries, oil, and gas pipelines	Generators
ICT	Investment in telecom lines and transmission towers	Equipment, including computers
Social infrastructure	Public utility buildings (schools, hospitals)	Human capital (e.g. teachers, nurses, doctors)
Housing and regional development	Low-income (social) housing	Luxury housing
Security and vital registration	Public utility buildings (police offices, barracks, fire stations)	Asset usage equipment (e.g. police cars, tanks)
Agriculture, water, and mining	Water treatment plants, sanitation plants Irrigation systems Rail and waterway mining infrastructure	Asset usage equipment (e.g. tractors, mining equipment)

supply and sewages, steel plants, electricity, petrochemical complexes, and facilities for information management. Under the transformation agenda document, infrastructure was defined as including transport, energy, information & communication technology (ICT), schools and hospitals, housing and regional development, agriculture, water and mining, and security and vital registration. The conceptualization of infrastructure is diagrammed in Table 6.2.

The first national implementation plan: 2012–2015

The first national implementation plan was founded on the transformation agenda document. The agenda aimed to deepen the effects and provide a sense of direction for the administration during the plan period. A baseline GDP growth rate of 11.7% per annum was assumed, translating to a real and nominal GDP of about USD428.6 billion and N73.2 trillion, respectively, at the end of the plan period in line with the policy target. A total investment of N40.75 trillion was projected by the end of the plan period.

The public sector was expected to invest about N24.45 trillion in this, and the private sector was expected to invest N16.3 trillion, representing 60% and 40%, respectively.

The projected GDP growth for the period was expected to come largely from oil and gas, solid minerals, agriculture, ICT equipment and software, telecommunications, wholesale and retail trade, tourism and entertainment, manufacturing, and building & construction. To realize the projected GDP growth, three key reforms were thought to be imperative, aimed at:

- Improving long-term economic growth and stability
- Improving the quality and quantum of Nigeria's infrastructure
- Enhancing the human capital development of Nigerians.

Priority policies, programs, and projects aligned with the key reforms were identified and selected in all sectors of the economy. Strategic policies, programs, and projects were implemented in the infrastructure sector to stimulate activities in the real sector and bring about the desired economic growth. Monitoring and evaluation mechanisms were put in place to track developments in policy and program performance.

Assessment of the first national implementation plan indicated that momentous success was recorded in the achievement of set goals. Four years after the launch of the transformation agenda document, Nigeria became the largest economy in Africa in terms of its gross domestic product (GDP), which stood at over $500 billion. During the plan period, the "national integrated infrastructure master plan", a blueprint for expanding and modernizing the nation's infrastructure over the next 30 years, was launched by President Jonathan (2010–2015) (Table 6.3).

During the first national implementation plan period (2012–2015), the local content policy in the oil and gas sector, which increased indigenous participation in the sector and created linkages to other sectors of the economy, led to the creation of more jobs for Nigerians in the oil and gas sector. The reformation of the transportation sector, by strengthening the legal framework for private sector participation, led to the ongoing construction of landmark infrastructure projects, including the construction of the second River Niger bridge in Onitsha, linking the eastern part of the country to the western part of the country, and the new Loko-Oweto bridge over the River Benue, linking the north-central part of the country to the eastern part. The dualization and rehabilitation of major north-south and east-west arterial roads, including Lagos-Ibadan-Ilorin-road, Benin--Ore-Sagamu road, Abuja-Lokoja-Benin road, Mokwa-Bida road, Kano-Potiskum-Maiduguri road, Onitsha-Owerri road, and Onitsha-Awka-Enugu-Port Harcout road, as well as the completion of the Nigeria-Cameroon segment of the Trans-African highway project (Enugu-Ogoja-Ikom-Mfum-Mbok road), among

Table 6.3 The budget for the first national implementation plan (first NIP)

Allocation by sector & MDAs under KPPP (2012–2015)	*2012 (N'million)*	*2013 (N'million)*	*2014 (N'million)*	*2015 (N'million)*	*Total 2012–2015 (N'million)*	*% Age share of total*
Real sector	2,28,519.80	2,51,450.73	2,67,722.37	2,72,562.77	10,20,255.67	14.17
– Agriculture & rural development	1,12,007.72	1,20,841.69	1,36,221.85	1,31,724.33	5,00,795.59	6.96
– Water resources	70,325.41	77,612.00	75,768.00	76,294.67	3,00,000.08	4.17
– Commerce & industry	14,534.90	16,156.17	16,413.36	16,975.56	64,080.00	0.89
– Mines & steel development	12,901.77	14,340.87	14,569.16	15,068.20	56,880.00	0.79
Physical infrastructure	4,19,550.00	4,79,680.00	5,40,310.00	5,83,980.00	20,23,520.00	28.10
– Transport	3,22,800.00	3,72,180.00	4,20,560.00	4,52,980.00	15,68,520.00	21.79
– Roads & bridges	1,50,000.00	1,70,000.00	1,85,000.00	1,90,500.00	6,95,500.00	9.66
– FERMA (for maintenance of roads)	45,300.00	55,150.00	74,550.00	75,000.00	2,50,000.00	3.47
– Ports	2,750.00	2,980.00	3,120.00	2,860.00	11,800.00	0.16
– Aviation (excluding BASA Funds)	35,000.00	45,850.00	17,500.00	14,320.00	1,12,670.00	1.56
– Railways	89,750.00	98,200.00	1,40,300.00	1,70,300.00	4,98,550.00	6.92
– Oil & gas	18,750.00	22,500.00	24,750.00	32,500.00	98,500.00	1.37
– Power	78,000.00	85,000.00	95,000.00	98,500.00	3,56,500.00	4.95
Regional development	2,29,113.71	2,43,315.74	1,93,186.77	1,74,922.65	8,40,538.87	11.67
– Housing	41,647.71	47,615.74	54,183.24	59,537.65	2,02,984.34	2.82
– Federal capital territory	1,42,446.00	1,05,700.00	35,600.00	4,004.00	2,87,770.00	4.00
– Niger Delta	45,000.00	90,000.00	1,03,403.53	1,11,381.00	3,49,784.53	4.86

Knowledge-based & ICT	17,155.48	25,314.61	32,485.98	38,500.00	1,13,456.07	1.58
Science and technology	13,060.00	20,555.00	27,505.00	38,500.00	99,620.00	1.38
Information communication technology	4,095.48	4,749.61	4,980.98	0	13,836.07	0.19
Human capital development	89,420.75	1,86,140.51	1,94,910.58	2,25,646.98	6,96,118.82	9.67
– Education	9,850.00	1,00,000.00	1,06,500.00	1,28,000.00	3,44,350.00	4.78
– Health	45,310.00	54,000.00	60,000.00	70,000.00	2,29,310.00	3.18
– Women & social development	7,103.45	7,519.03	7,129.33	6,619.58	28,371.39	0.39
– Youth development	11,833.61	10,270.42	6,285.14	6,812.41	35,201.58	0.49
– Labor & productivity	15,323.69	14,351.06	14,996.11	14,214.99	58,885.85	0.82
General administration	50,077.42	55,986.32	57,357.45	60,841.92	2,24,263.11	3.11
Defense & security	1,69,846.06	1,88,791.21	1,91,796.57	1,98,366.15	7,48,800.00	10.40
Grand total	12,03,683.23	14,30,679.12	14,77,769.72	15,54,820.47	56,66,952.54	78.71
Government contribution to bankable projects					9,11,660.00	12.66
Funds for other priority projects not listed					6,21,387.46	8.63
Total funds available					72,00,000.00	100.00

others, was laudable. The Abuja-Kaduna new standard-gauge rail line segment recorded about 90 percent completion during the plan period.

In the agriculture sector, the government ended its participation in the production and distribution of fertilizer and seeds, and developed value chains in agricultural priority areas, such as rice, cassava, livestock, and fisheries. This resulted in farmers having increased access to inputs and expanded the domestic production of fertilizer leading to reduction in food importation bill, from 1.4 trillion naira in 2009 to 684 billion naira by December 2013.

The national industrial revolution plan aimed at driving agricultural processing industries, metals and solid minerals development, and oil & gas-related fabrications and light manufacturing led to a new national automotive policy. This led to the establishment of new vehicle assembly plants, resulting in the ability of Nigerian companies to manufacture vehicles again and stemming capital flights due to massive importation of vehicles. This led to the creation of more jobs in the country.

The sovereign wealth fund established during the plan period not only provided enough buffers for government when the prices of oil crashed but also led other private equity firms in infrastructure development initiatives, including the second Niger bridge project.

The introduction of the treasury single account (TSA) in 2012, intended to unify the structure of the government bank account, led to better management of the government's cash flow. The integrated payroll system (IPPIS) tackled the problem of ghost workers and curtailed rising recurrent expenditure, leading to the discovery of 60,450 ghost workers in the federal government and resulting in savings of about 185 billion naira, which was now directed to infrastructure projects.

The Jonathan administration reforms and the implementation of the first national implementation plan of vision 20:2020 consolidated Nigeria's economic growth and stability, generating private sector investments in infrastructure that supported growth in the real sectors of the economy. It was expected that the second national implementation plan (2016–2020) will consolidate and build on the gains of the first national implementation plan (2011–2015).

Funding implementation plans

A comparison between the projected expenditure under the first national implementation plan's key policies, programs, and projects (KPPP), and the budget provision for the sectors would indicate a considerable shortfall in the projected sectoral investments. For example, the physical infrastructure sector, encompassing roads and rails, and the power, oil, and gas sectors, for which about N2 trillion expenditure was planned, only had a budgetary provision of about N800 billion for the plan period, representing about 40% of the planned expenditure. This indicates a shortfall of 60%.

This shortfall in projected expenditure points to difficulties in realizing the goals of the first national implementation plan. The situation was further exacerbated by the poor actual releases of budgeted funds for the projects, which, under the plan period (2012–2015), stood at an average of about 65%, at best. This indicated a compliance rate of about only 25% of the projected sectoral expenditure under the first implementation plan.

This misalignment of the budgetary revenue and development plan is symptomatic of poor infrastructure development in Nigeria. It also indicates a lack of fiscal fidelity to development plans, which has been the bane of development planning in Nigeria since 1970.

Summary

Chapter 6 has been devoted to a review of Vision 20:2020 because of its significant place in the story of infrastructure development in Nigeria. The vision, pillars, and strategic objectives have been diagrammed, and the Transformation Agenda shows the guiding principles. At the core of Vision 20:2020 are the implementation plans, with their detailed budgets and timelines. There is great confidence that the vision to make Nigeria one of the top 20 economies by 2020 will inspire both the leadership and the citizens for the next few years.

Bibliography

Babatunde, S. O., Opawole, A., & Akinsiku, O. E. (2012). Critical success factors in public-private partnership (PPP) on infrastructure delivery in Nigeria. *Journal of Facilities Management, 10*(3), 212–225. doi:10.1108/14725961211246018

Dahiru, D., Abdul Azeez, A. D., & Bala, K. (2013). *Study of measures for enhancing public-private partnership towards infrastructure development in Nigeria*. Conference Paper on Sustainable Building. Coventry University. Retrieved from www.coventry.ac.uk/Global/Faculty%20events/SB13/SB13–42-Study-of-measures-for-enhancing-public-private-partnership-towards-infrastructural-development-in-Nigeria.pdf

Federal Government of Nigeria. (2010). The millennium development goals (MDGs) report. Retrieved from www.undp.org/content/dam/undp/libray/MDG/english/MDG

Gwilliam, K. (2011). *Africa's transport infrastructure: Mainstreaming maintenance and management*. Washington, DC: The World Bank.

Idris, A., Kura, S. M., & Bashir, M. U. (2013). Public private partnership in Nigeria and improvement in service delivery: An appraisal. *Journal of Humanities and Social Sciences, 10*(3), 63–71. Retrieved from www.Iosrjournals.org

Iroghama, P. I. (2012). Trust in government: A note from Nigeria. *International Journal of Academic Research in Economics and Management Sciences, 2*(1), 258–267. Retrieved from http://hrmars.com/admin/pics/857.pdf

Jonathan, G. (2015). *Innovative reforms of President Goodluck Jonathan's administration* (pp. 17–24). Abuja: The Office of the Chief Economic Adviser to the President.

Kemp, R., Parto, S., & Gibson, R. B. (2005). Governance for sustainable development: Moving from theory to practice. *International Journal of Sustainable Development, 8*(1/2), 12–30. doi:10.1504/IJSD.2005.007372

Lawal, T., & Oluwatoyin, A. (2011). National development in Nigeria: Issues, challenges and prospects. *Journal of Public Administration and Policy Research, 3*(9), 237–241. doi:10.5897/JPAR11.012

Marcellus, I. C. (2009). Development planning in Nigeria: Reflections on the national economic empowerment and development strategies (NEEDS) 2003–2007. *Journal of Social Sciences, 20*(30), 197–210.

Mbanefo, C. A. (2000). The role of engineering infrastructure in national development. In M. D. Abdullahi (Ed.), *Provision & maintenance of engineering infrastructure for technological development in Nigeria* (pp. 37–44). Kaduna: Fahimta Publishing Company.

National Planning Commission. (2007). National report. The presidency, federal republic of Nigeria.

National Planning Commission. (2009). Nigeria Vision 20:2020 Economic Transformation Blueprint. The presidency, federal republic of Nigeria.

National Planning Commission. (2015). National integrated infrastructure master plan. The presidency, federal republic of Nigeria.

Naswem, A. A., Okwoche, V. A., & Age, A. I. (2016). Mainstreaming sustainability in the Nigerian agricultural transformation agenda. *World, 3*(1), 054–059.

Natsa, R. (2015). *Nigeria: As FG launches ATA-SP Phase 1*. All Africa. Retrieved from http://allafrica.com/stories/201503130138.html

Nwanolue, B. O. G., & Iwuoha, V. C. (2012). The Nigerian civil service and promotion of sustainable human development: A critical analysis. *Arabian Journal of Business and Management Review, 1*(9), 12–21. Retrieved from www.arabianjbmr.com

Obadan, M. I. (2003). *National development planning and budgeting in Nigeria: Some pertinent issues*. Lagos: Broadway Press Limited.

Ogbonna, B. C. (2012). Structural adjustment program (SAP) in Nigeria. An empirical assessment. *Journal of Banking, 6*(1), 19–40. Retrieved from www.academia.edu/

Ogu, V. I. (2000). Stakeholders' partnership approach to infrastructure provision and management in developing world cities: Lessons from the sustainable Ibadan project. *Human Settlement Development, 111*, 1–18. doi:10.1016/S0197-3975(00)00015-1

Okonjo-Iweala, N. (2012). *Reforming the unreformable: Lessons from Nigeria*. Cambridge, MA: The MIT Press.

Okonjo-Iweala, N., & Osafo-Kwaako, P. (2007). Nigeria's economic reforms: Progress and challenges. Retrieved from www.brokings.edu/research/papers/200

Okotoni, O. (2001). Problems and prospects of Nigerian bureaucracy. *Journal of Social Sciences, 7*(3), 223–229. Retrieved from http://thescipub.com/jss.toc

Olaopa, T. (2010). *Public service reforms in Africa*. Ibadan: University Press Plc.

Olaseni, M., & Alade, W. (2012). Vision 20:2020 and the challenges of infrastructure development in Nigeria. *Journal of Sustainable Development, 5*(2), 1–14. doi:10.5539/jsd.v5n2p63

Olumide, H. A. (2011). Telecommunication reform and effects of competition on availability, quality and cost of services in Nigeria. *Public Policy and Administration Research, 1*(3), 8–20. Retrieved from www.iist.org/Journals/index.php/PPAR

Songi, O. (2008). *Electoral reform in Nigeria: Prospects and challenges.* Retrieved from http//works.bepress.com

Taye, O. O., & Dada, M. O. (2012). Appraisal of private sector involvement in infrastructure development in Lagos, Nigeria. *Mediterranean Journal of Social Sciences, 3*(2), 399–412. doi:10.5901/mjss.2012.v3n2.399

Udoka, C. A., & Anyingang, R. A. (2012). The effects of privatization on economic growth on Nigeria: 1979–2007 in retrospect. *International Journal of Economic Development, Research and Investment, 3*(2), 25–35. Retrieved from www.icidr.org/

UNDP. (1997). Reconceptualizing governance. Discussion paper 2, Management Development and Governance.

7 Corruption and other obstacles to infrastructure development

Corruption in Nigeria

Corruption has deeply permeated Nigerian society. In the Transparency International Corruption Perception Index of 1995–1997, Nigeria was named the most corrupt nation in the world. The indices of 2001, 2010, and 2013 confirmed this status.

The corruption perception index has been used as a global barometer for measuring corruption as well as a yardstick for good governance by the World Bank Group and the Forum for New World Governance. In these indices, the level of corruption in Nigeria has been adjudged as disturbingly high. Its citizens generally believe that government officials are corrupt and that corruption is at the heart of the deprivation, unemployment, poverty, and social insecurity that remain unabated in the country.

Categorization of corruption in Nigeria

Corruption in Nigeria can be grouped into three categories:

- **Political corruption:** This occurs at the highest level of the political spectrum and involves politicians and political decision-makers engaged in the distortion and manipulation of the processes and institutions of governance.
- **Bureaucratic corruption:** This occurs in public places on daily basis among public officials and ordinary people.
- **Electoral corruption:** This includes vote buying and all electoral malpractices involving the exchange of money in the process of rigging an election.

The other forms of corrupt practice in Nigeria include bribery, fraudulent activities, embezzlement of public funds, and extortion. Notable among corrupt practices in Nigeria is the infamous "419" scam that gave the nation an ugly international image. Scam artists claiming to be Nigerian royalty promised riches in return for a small payment. "419" is the number of the article in the Nigerian Criminal Code that makes this kind of fraud illegal, although, in fact, the scam did not always originate in Nigeria. Other kinds of fraud include oil theft, popularly known as "illegal bunkering", and billions of dollars of public funds stolen by political leaders. Due to decades of widespread corruption, Nigeria's educational and social systems, as well as key infrastructure, such as roads, railways, electrical power, and refineries have suffered tremendous setbacks. It is useful to examine the phenomenon of corruption and the reasons why it has been so endemic in Nigeria, with a focus on bureaucratic corruption.

Dimensions of corruption

Corruption can be broadly defined as a perversion or a violation of established rules. It has been made manifest in the total misuse of public power for private gains. Viewed as anti-social behavior, it assumes the ugly images of embezzlement and misappropriation of public funds and resources, bribery, fraudulent practices, and extortion. There are two distinguishable forms of corruption in Nigeria:

- State-orchestrated corruption through bureaucratic machinery of government
- Corruption within the social fabric of the society

A clear distinction has been made between state-centric corruption that involves the bureaucratic machinery of the state and the culture of corruption that focuses on more pervasive forms of societal impropriety. The poor state of infrastructure in Nigeria is attributable to bureaucratic corruption and fueled by a lack of good governance and transparency, unethical behavior by bureaucrats, near-absent ethical governance in the public service, non-transparent procurement processes, inadequate training of public officials, and inadequate monitoring and evaluation systems at the implementation stage of infrastructure development. Generally, corruption can best be visualized as a conscious attempt to divert public resources from the satisfaction of the general interest to that of a selfish personal interest.

Causes of corruption

Some factors have been identified as the root causes of corruption, especially in developing countries like Nigeria. These include:

- Inequality in wealth distribution
- Political office as the primary means of gaining access to wealth
- Conflict between changing moral codes
- The weaknesses of social and governmental enforcement mechanisms
- The absence of a keen sense of national community
- Greed
- Insatiable appetite for wealth

- Complete disregard for the rule of law
- Lack of altruism
- Impunity
- The get-rich-quick syndrome
- Diminished moral values
- Winner-takes-all attitude
- Provocative displays of affluence and ill-gotten wealth
- Lack of sanctions for perpetrators of corruption
- Extreme poverty rate
- Lack of patriotism

Bureaucratic corruption

Bureaucracy is the institutional mechanism for carrying out the functions and responsibilities of the state, and it is the vehicle for political and economic administration of a country. The bureaucracy which is based on hierarchy, rules, regulations, and orders helps to translate the vision of the leadership into reality. Public officers who work in a bureaucracy are referred to as bureaucrats, and their actions either promote or hinder good governance. In Nigeria, bureaucratic corruption is usually associated with the activities of bureaucrats and takes the form of buying favor from bureaucrats who formulate and implement government policies.

> Several reasons have been advanced for the prevalence of bureaucratic corruption in Nigeria. Those reasons include the innocuous bureaucratic structure of the public service, lack of value, unethical practices and penchant for pecuniary gains. It can be said that bureaucratic corruption is an obstacle to good governance and poses a serious threat to efficient management of resources and improvement in the well-being of the people. Bureaucratic corruption, coupled with poor leadership, has been blamed for the slow pace of development of infrastructure in key sectors of the Nigerian economy.

Bureaucratic corruption occurs in public institutions, ministries, departments, and agencies of government, usually between public officials and citizens in the process of delivering services to other citizens, and between public officials and private sector operators engaged in government contracts and projects. Bureaucratic corruption is the most visible type of corruption in Nigeria.

The Nigerian Bureau of Statistics (2017) revealed in its national corruption report, covering the period between June 2015 and May 2016, that about N400 billion (approximately $4.6 billion), representing about 40% of the combined federal and state education budgets in 2016, is paid out as bribes to public officials in Nigeria every year. The report, prepared in collaboration with the United Nations Office on Drugs and Crime (UNODC), pointed out that bribery is an established part of administrative procedure in Nigeria, and law enforcement agencies are the biggest bribe-takers. Public officials often initiate bribery directly or indirectly, and about 70% of bribes are paid upfront before a service is rendered.

The magnitude of public sector bribery in Nigeria assumes a cancerous dimension when one realizes that the average bribe payer in Nigeria pays an average of six bribes annually. According to the report, bribery is prevalent not only in the public sector but also in the private sector. Surprised by the level of corruption among those entrusted with political authority and public funds, Okonjo-Iweala (2012, p. 84) noted:

> Most accounts of corruption in Nigeria pale in comparison with the brazen corruption of General Sani Abacha, Nigeria's military ruler from 1993 to 1998.

A corruption-free bureaucracy in Nigeria will create a favorable climate for investment, economic growth, and social stability. Experts agree that there is a relationship between infrastructural decay in Nigeria and bureaucratic corruption, and argue that, beyond lack of funds, corruption is the main cause of the level of infrastructural decay in Nigeria. Bureaucratic corruption has not only deprived the Nigerian people of good infrastructure but has also distorted incentives, undermined institutions, and redistributed wealth and power to the undeserving without adding value to the nation's economy.

Many political leaders in Nigeria have attempted to institute some form of anti-corruption measures, such as the War Against Indiscipline (WAI) of 1983–1985, executive and legislative actions that led to the enactment of the Independent Corrupt Practices Commission (ICPC) in 2000, the Economic and Financial Crimes Commission (EFCC) in 2003, and the Public Procurement Act (PPA) in 2007. These institutions were geared towards fighting bureaucratic corruption.

Despite these anti-corruption measures, bureaucratic corruption continues to exacerbate and deepen in Nigeria, placing a huge barrier on the path to individual rights to liberty, equality, justice, and national development. Corruption has been blamed for the failure of the nation to provide employment, eradicate poverty, develop infrastructure, and institute good public governance. It has been argued that corruption; lack of political will; nepotism; and the absence of integrity, accountability, and transparency are partly responsible for the failure of past development plans in Nigeria.

Corruption and public trust

Many Nigerian citizens believe that all levels of government officials are corrupt and have vested interests in most public procurements, which affects their performance in the good governance of infrastructure development. This has led to a prevailing lack of trust among citizens in the government and in bureaucrats engaged in the delivery of infrastructure and services to the public.

The infrastructure sector in Nigeria has been associated with corruption and corrupt practices. Estimates of financial losses range between 10% and 30% of the total value of publicly funded construction projects (Transparency International, 2013). Most infrastructure projects in Nigeria have been abandoned or failed due to bureaucratic corruption. In a study of project failure in Nigeria, corruption, lack of professionalism, inexperienced project managers/project personnel, and flawed bureaucratic procurement processes were identified as the main causes. Infrastructural decay can also be traced to corruption and lack of accountability and transparency among bureaucratic office holders. Notably, accountability and transparency are vital indicators of good governance, that could help to engender public trust, and contribute immensely to infrastructure development.

Impact of corruption on growth

Corruption and poor governance affect growth and public service delivery in Nigeria. In such a corrupt environment, resources for human capital development and investments in infrastructure, health, and education are diverted, leading to a deepening of poverty among the poor. To combat corruption, two economic reform strategies are imperative:

- Embedding anti-corruption education in a comprehensive reform program that should be embedded in schools' curriculum, places of worship and among various communities of citizens.
- Conducting diagnostic studies to identify specific areas in which corruption had a highly negative impact on public welfare

The effect of corruption on good governance

The reality is that the magnitude of corruption in Nigeria, especially bureaucratic corruption, has made good governance practically impossible. There is widespread misuse of public power for private gains, which is an indicator of the extent to which the Nigerian political system has become dysfunctional.

> Good governance cannot be attained in a chronically corrupt political leadership structure, because corruption violates public trust and deviates from high moral standards in exchange or anticipation of pecuniary gains at the expense of the common good.

Other obstacles to infrastructure development

Nigeria has enacted many development plans and other long-term, medium-term, and short-term plans aimed at achieving defined macroeconomic goals and objectives with multi-faceted economic and social benefits to citizens.

These plans ought to have led to the development of good infrastructure in the country. However, only the first national development plan (1962–1968) achieved its main objectives. The distinguishing factors between the plan and those that followed it were its realistic nature, as well as its alignment with the yearly national budgets. From 1969 onward, Nigeria failed to produce the much-needed sustainable development due mainly to a lack of good infrastructure in every sector of the nation's economy. Yet it has been observed that developing countries that are consistent with development planning as a development strategy, such as India and the "Asian Tigers", have achieved macroeconomic stability, higher export revenues, higher disposable income, greatly improved life expectancy, and overall structural transformation of their societies in the long run.

The example of India, which adopted development planning as a strategy for national development in 1960 (the same year Nigeria adopted a development planning strategy), is instructive. India has implemented 12 five-year development plans consistently. This has led to high confidence in local and foreign investors, attracting public-private partnership investments of about 480 billion dollars in the 12th plan (2011–2015) alone, with an additional one trillion dollars investment committed by the private sector in the 13th development plan (2016–2020).

In Chapter 5, we saw the inconsistency in the adoption of development planning strategy in Nigeria. Despite the series of development plans introduced by governments after 1968, the country failed to achieve its goals due to unrealistic, vague, and unmeasurable development plans as well as other obstacles, which we will discuss next.

Political instability and the Nigerian civil war

Political instability and the Nigerian civil war were major obstacles to infrastructure development. Between 1960 and 2015, Nigerians witnessed 13 government regime changes. Several military coups disrupted its continuity of governance and infrastructure development. Government projects, such as roads, rails, metrolines, housing, power, and steel plants, that had been under construction were either abandoned or their contracts revoked by succeeding administrations for no justifiable reasons. Political interference created uncertainty and stifled the process of bureaucratic decision making, which, in turn, affected infrastructure development.

During the Nigerian Civil War, between 1967 and 1970, resources were diverted to the war effort, at the expense of infrastructure development. In fact, the civil war resulted in the destruction of what little infrastructure there was. For example, the new river Niger bridge, built and commissioned by the Balewa government in 1964, was destroyed during the war, thereby severing the link between the western and eastern parts of the country. After the war, there was a slow recovery effort, a part of which was rebuilding infrastructural facilities, such as roads, bridges, telecommunication, and power. The effect of the war on infrastructure development is still visible today in some parts of Nigeria.

> Political instability acts as a disincentive to private sector investors and leads to loss of confidence in the economy, denying the economy of investment in infrastructure development through public-private partnerships.

The military coup and regime change in 1966

The military coup of 1966, which took place about four years after the commencement of Nigeria's first national development plan, adversely affected development planning more than any other coup. It resulted in the abrogation of the healthy political and fiscal relationship between Nigeria's central government and its four regional governments, which had led to the formulation and implementation of the first national development plan and its positive and commensurate results and achievements. It is believed that economic and physical development would have been enhanced in Nigeria if the military had not interfered in its political governance.

In place of the republican government that had existed in Nigeria from 1963 to 1966, the military introduced a political and fiscal unitary system that was in sync with military command and control. Under the regional system, regions had their own constitutions, distinct from the constitution of the federal government, and had control over their own resources, exploiting those resources and retaining about 60% of the income generated therefrom while contributing the remaining 40% to a central pool controlled by the federal government. This led to the development of critical infrastructure in all four regions, quite apart from what the federal government was doing on infrastructure development.

However, the loss of autonomy by the four regions was followed by the establishment of administrative units called states, created arbitrarily by the military in a manner that was not compatible with the four-regional structure. There was no longer motivation for arduous work since the states no longer retained 60% of the revenue generated from their exploitation of mineral and agricultural resources in their territories. As a result, states received allocations from the federal government, which, by military decree, appropriated all their mineral resources to itself. This led to the erosion of the capacity of the regions/states to embark on major infrastructure development in the way they had prior to 1966, when the military first seized power in Nigeria. The current system of "unitary federalism" that assigns all natural resources and revenues derived therefrom to the federal government, which, in turn, gives "handouts" to the states, is inimical to good governance of infrastructure development, and is at the core of lack of good governance in Nigeria.

Unskilled manpower, funding constraints, and material resources

The implementation of government policies, plans, and projects on infrastructure development has been hampered by funding constraints and lack of skilled manpower and material resources. Successive administrations in Nigeria have relied heavily on foreign loans as a critical source of funding for infrastructure development projects, resulting in a huge amount of foreign debt, totaling over 40 billion dollars by 1999.

Revenue generated from oil exports proved inadequate to fund all infrastructure and development programs, including agriculture, education, rural development, and the provision of social amenities. Most material resources needed for infrastructure development in Nigeria are imported from overseas, including bitumen for highway construction and iron and steel for bridges, railways, and housing projects. In addition, Nigeria relies on foreign construction companies to execute major infrastructure projects. Human and material resources are lacking in most areas of the construction industry, particularly in engineering works, such as road construction, telecommunications, and electrical power production. A comprehensive approach toward these challenges that will leverage on local resources and manpower has been advocated.

Lack of continuity in policy and implementation

Lack of continuity in government plans, policies, programs, and projects has been the bane of infrastructure development in Nigeria. Quite often, development plans and programs are abandoned once the government that has put them in place leaves office. New programs, often not compatible with the original plan objectives, are introduced, with negative impact on initial goals. The situation has been worsened by the spate of regime changes and political instability that the country has witnessed since 1966, when the first military coup and change of government took place. Even without changes in government, policy somersaults have also led to a lack of continuity in policies, programs, and projects as well as their implementation.

Lack of discipline

The failure of political leaders and bureaucrats to abide by development plan objectives has, in the past, frustrated development plans in Nigeria. Most early development plans became distorted at the implementation stage, which led to the non-realization of their objectives. The lack of discipline often exhibited at this stage led to many abandoned projects in various parts of the country. Projects such as the Ajaokuta Steel Complex, Ikot Abasi Aluminum Smelter Plant, and the various steel rolling mills, which should have catalyzed Nigeria's industrialization, remained incomplete about two decades after their scheduled completion dates. Robust project management training is required to equip bureaucrats with the skills and discipline required for them to realize plan objectives.

Ineffective public-private partnership

There has been poor collaboration between the public and private sectors in delivering infrastructure projects in Nigeria. Bureaucrats often see infrastructure projects as their exclusive domain and don't see private sector players as trustworthy. Booby traps are sometimes put in the way of private sector players to frustrate them and drive them out, paving the way for the traditional award of contracts, considered more beneficial to corrupt bureaucrats. On the other hand, private sector players see bureaucrats as corrupting the process of awarding contracts and as being responsible for contract failures. Due to this lack of public confidence and the prevailing mutual suspicion between the public and private sectors in Nigeria, the public-private partnership paradigm is still in its infancy, many years after it was first mooted. This has led to huge capital flight from the country by some private sector players, who prefer to invest in other countries, where their capital is adjudged safe and welcome.

Lack of commitment

Development plans are often prepared without consultation with the people. Sometimes, there is also not enough consultation with the organized private sector that is expected to make material contributions to the plans. When citizens and private sector investors have not participated at the formulation stage, and are therefore not acquainted with the plan details, they become apathetic and do not claim ownership of the plan. Not surprisingly, they are therefore not motivated to work towards the plan's success.

Lack of good governance

The inability of Nigeria's government to adequately tackle most developmental challenges, such as poverty, unemployment, security, and the deplorable state of infrastructure, has been attributed to lack of good governance. Good governance is inclusive and focuses on maximizing the benefits to citizens through a more effective and efficient use of public resources, good fiscal management, and financial prudence in the development of infrastructure, while providing opportunities to citizens to be gainfully engaged in productive ventures.

For example, despite many citizens of Nigeria suffering from poor electricity supply, the Mambilla hydro powerplant that was conceived in 1982, with a capacity to generate over 3,050 MW of electricity in the first phase, and ramping up to about 10,000 MW at full completion with capacity to produce about 4.7 billion KWH of electricity was abandoned after initial construction began and progressed satisfactorily. This is a clear example of lack of good governance. In the about four decades this hydro powerplant has been abandoned, billions of dollars have been lost. That money represents what would have been added to the country's GDP if the power plant had since been completed and commissioned, and used to supply constant electricity to manufacturing plants and businesses in parts of Nigeria.

Poor budgeting

Poor budgeting practices, including non-alignment of capital budgets with development and other strategic plans, coupled with poor funding, as experienced periodically in Nigeria, remain key obstacles to infrastructure development. For example, under the First National Implementation Plan (referred to in Chapter 6), roads and bridges were expected to attract a budget of 190.5 billion naira in 2015. However, the budget under this heading in 2015 was a paltry 18 billion naira, less than 10% of the expected plan provision. As such, only little progress would have been made in this project execution in 2015. Such a huge misalignment between fiscal allocation and development plan can only lead to project failure.

> Expenditure on development projects, public goods and public services through development-based budgeting is advantageous. It provides a solid base for synchronizing set objectives and goals for development plans and other strategic initiatives in various sectors of the economy, and allows for the monitoring of progress, both in project planning and implementation on a regular basis.

Most state and national budgets have huge sums of money for "security vote" meant for the protection of the state governors, and the president, respectively, while infrastructure get meagre allocations, which are far less than security votes for the executives. Such humongous security votes have been the source of corruption at the executive level, where funds that should have gone into infrastructure development are frittered away.

Lack of monitoring and evaluation

Absence of routine monitoring and evaluation has adversely affected infrastructure development in Nigeria, leading to the abandonment of projects. Monitoring and evaluation are authentic project management tools used for tracking developments in policy and program performance as well as project execution. To succeed, infrastructure projects need to measure inputs, outputs, outcomes, and the impact of policies, programs, and projects on the economy and welfare of citizens.

Political interference in contract procurement

Interference by political leadership is one of the major causes of corruption in the bureaucracy. Often, once leadership is interested in a contract, the rules are suspended, and the processes are compromised. This could lead to major corruption, which sometimes includes inflation of contract costs, engagement of incompetent contractors, inflation of invoices, delays in contract execution, abandonment of contract/project, and contract/project failure.

Political interference was rampant during the military administrations because there were no checks and balances. As a result, corruption was at an all-time high during the era of military dictatorship. Many infrastructure projects were awarded without competitive bidding, sometimes by military fiat. In some cases, contractors designed the projects and dictated the cost, which often were inflated. Arbitrariness in project conception, design, costing, and execution was the order of the day.

However, President Yaradua's administration introduced the Public Procurement Act in 2007, which brought about transparency in contracts award and in the privatization and commercialization of government enterprises. The new transparent procurement processes, which include stringent prequalification processes, usually weed out incompetent contractors. This has led to increased standardization and reduced the kind of illegal practices that had been widespread in the past. A climate of zero tolerance for corruption, probity, accountability, and transparency now prevail in the government's infrastructure projects.

Political and bureaucratic interference in budgeting

Political interference during the yearly budgeting process has also led to the failure of infrastructure development in Nigeria. At the budget consideration stage, bureaucrats introduce projects that often have no bearing on the development plan. Members of the national assembly (legislators) have been found to introduce new or constituency projects that do not align with the national development plan. This has led to frequent altercations between the executive and legislative arms of government, resulting in the late passage of national budgets, with adverse consequences for infrastructure development. Between 2005 and 2015, about 100 billion naira have been devoted to constituency projects yearly, thereby short-changing critical projects that are aligned with plan objectives. This phenomenon is inimical to the concept of development planning.

Poor leadership and lack of political will

Poor leadership and lack of political will have been partly responsible for the poor state of infrastructure in Nigeria. In the past, political leaders have failed to take ownership of the development and strategic plans they inherited from past governments and muster the political will needed for the implementation of these plans. The success of any developing economy depends, to some extent, on its adherence to planning, and purposeful implementation of plans, with the leadership driving the process and ensuring compliance. Political leaders in Nigeria have been reluctant to play this role. Not much can be achieved in terms of infrastructure development if the leaders do not offer support to projects aimed at the common good and resolve bottlenecks as they appear.

Ineffective public service

The public service is the bureaucracy for carrying out the functions of the state, and it is central to the development process as it is responsible for the implementation of development plans. The Nigerian public service has historically been weak, untrained, and corrupt, leading to poor governance of infrastructure development. Proactive engagement against corruption in the public service, and holding bureaucrats accountable to the rules of procedure and process, should be considered and adopted. Project officers should be given the requisite training before they are sent to supervise development projects.

Poor remuneration

Bureaucrats in Nigeria are poorly remunerated, and yet they are expected to administer various projects, costing billions of naira. In a highly demoralized environment where merit is not rewarded, and job security is not guaranteed, most bureaucrats tend to circumvent the system. They make compromises for financial gain, to the detriment of the common good, sometimes leading to inflation of contract budgets or outright connivance with contractors.

For example, before 1999, a deputy director earned about N60,000 per month, but they were saddled with managing projects totaling billions of naira. The probability that such a public officer would engage in corruption to meet his responsibilities to his family and society, and to guarantee his financial security upon retirement from the public service, was high. Some civil servants in Nigeria live above their means, by compromising the system, and this situation has dire consequences for infrastructure development.

Summary

How has corruption interfered with Nigerian infrastructure development over the years? Chapter 7 has pointed to the ways in which the behavior of corrupt leaders and bureaucrats added to the corruption and led to the destruction of policies and programs, with the result that infrastructure that would have helped the economy and reduced poverty and many social issues fell victim to the greed of those in power. In addition to corruption, we listed many other barriers to infrastructure development, from diverting funds away from planned projects to ineffective and self-serving civil services. Having named these problems, we will now turn our attention to some of the strategies that may contribute to resolving them.

Bibliography

Achebe, C. (1988). *The trouble with Nigeria.* Enugu: Fourth Dimension Publishers.

Adenugba, A. A. (2013). Good governance and accountability in Nigeria's development dilemma. *Mediterranean Journal of Social Sciences, 4*(2). Retrieved from www.mcser.org/journal/index.php/mjss/article/view/267

Adeyeri, S. (2013). Conflicts and political instability in Nigeria; A critical discourse. *International Journal of Advanced Research in Management and Social Sciences, 2*(10), 119–130. Retrieved from www.academia.edu

Afegbua, I. A. (2010). Conflicts and political instability in Nigeria: Causes, consequences and prospects. *Journal of Social Science and Public Policy,* 2, 10–18. Retrieved from www.cenresin.org

Anigbogu, N. A., & Shwarka, M. S. (2011). Evaluation of the impact of the public procurement reform program on combating corrupt practices in public building projects delivery in Nigeria. *Environtech Journal, 1*(2), 43–51. Retrieved from www.google.com

Bouchat, C. J. (2013). The causes of instability in Nigeria and implications for the United States. Retrieved from www.strategicStudiesInstitute.army.mil/

Deloitte Global Series. (2012). Public governance and accountability. Retrieved from www.deloitte.com

Dike, V. (2008). Corruption in Nigeria: A new paradigm for effective control. *Africa Economic Analysis,* 1–17. Retrieved from www.africaeconomicanalysis.org

Egwemi, V. (2012). Corruption and corrupt practices in Nigeria: An agenda for taming the monster. *Journal of Sustainable Development in Africa, 14*(3), 72–85. Retrieved from www.jsd-africa.com/Jsda/

Ekpenkhio, S. A. (2003). *Public sector procurement reforms: The Nigerian experience.* Conference Paper. Nigeria. Retrieved from www.wto.org

Ezeh, E. M. (2013). Public procurement reform strategies. Retrieved from https://cips.org/Documents/Engr.%20Emeka%20Ezeh%20presentation%20%2821%20May%29%20%5BRepaired%5D.pdf

Fagbadebo, O. (2007). Corruption, governance and political instability in Nigeria. *African Journal of Political Science and International Relations, 1*(2), 28–37. Retrieved from www.academicjournals.org/AJPSIR

Hawkins, J. (2013). *How to note: Reducing corruption in infrastructure sector.* Conference Paper

Iroghama, P. I. (2012). Trust in government: A note from Nigeria. *International Journal of Academic Research in Economics and Management Sciences, 2*(1), 258–267. Retrieved from http://hrmars.com/admin/pics/857.pdf

Lawal, G., & Tobi, A. (2006). Bureaucratic corruption, good governance and development: The challenges and prospects of institution building in Nigeria.

Journal of Applied Sciences Research, 2(10), 642–649. Retrieved from www.aensiweb.com/jasr.html

Mustapha, M. (2010). Corruption in Nigeria: Conceptual and empirical notes. *Information, Society and Justice, 3*(2), 165–175. Retrieved from www.londonmet.ac.uk

National Bureau of Statistics. (2017). National corruption report. Retrieved from www.unodc.org/documents/data-and-analysis/Crime-statistics/Nigeria/Corruption_Nigeria_2017_07_31_web.pdf

Ogbeidi, M. M. (2012). Political leadership and corruption in Nigeria since 1960: A socioeconomic analysis. *Journal of Nigerian Studies, 1*(2), 1–25. Retrieved from www.unh.edu/nigerianstudies/articles/Issue2/Political_leadership.pdf

Okekeocha, C. (2013). *A case study of corruption and public accountability in Nigeria.* A Practicum Paper for M.A. Degree, Kennesaw State University.

Okonjo-Iweala, N. (2012). *Reforming the unreformable: Lessons from Nigeria.* Cambridge, MA: The MIT Press.

Onolememen, M. O. (2015). *The impact of leadership on the governance of infrastructure development in Nigeria* (Doctoral dissertation). Walden University, Minneapolis, MN.

Rotberg, R. I. (2005). Strengthening governance: Ranking countries would help. *The Washington Quarterly, 28*(1), 71–81. doi:10.1162/0163660042518215

Songi, O. (2008). *Electoral reform in Nigeria: Prospects and challenges.* Retrieved from http//works.bepress.com

Therkildsen, O. (2001). *Efficiency, accountability and implementation: Public sector reforms in East and Southern Africa.* Democracy, Governance and Human Rights; UNRISD. Retrieved from www.unrisd.org

Transparency International. (2010). *Corruption perceptions index.* Retrieved from www.transparency.org/cpi2010/results

Transparency International. (2013). *Transparency and accountability. United States Agency for International Development (USAID).* Retrieved from www.usaid.gov/pdf_docs/PDACP977.pdf

Transparency International. (2014). *Nigeria: Corruption and insecurity.* Retrieved from www.transparency.org/news/feature/nigeria_corruption_and_insecurity

World Bank Group. (2002). *Nigeria governance and corruption diagnostic study.* Analysis of survey results. Final Report. Nigeria. Retrieved from www.theijst.com/force_download.php?file_path=wp-content/uploads/2017/

UNDP. (1997). Reconceptualizing governance. Discussion paper 2, Management Development and Governance.

United Nations. (2007). *Public governance indicators: A literature review.* Retrieved from http://unpan1.un.org

Zuofa, T., & Ochieng, E. G. (2014). Project failure: The way forward and panacea for development. *International Journal of Business and Management, 9*(11), 59–71. Retrieved from www.ccsenet.org/ijbm

8 Strategies for infrastructure development

The infrastructure challenge

In the past decade, Nigeria's economy has grown by an average of 6.5% annually, driven largely by revenue receipts from sales of crude oil, the country's main revenue earner. These revenue receipts have been partly devoted to funding the country's consumption-led growth model, rather than investment-led growth model which should have been able to deliver good infrastructure development to Nigerians. Nigeria became the largest economy in Africa in 2014. The country not only possessed the continent's largest and one of the fastest-growing domestic markets at the time, it also contributed to about 30% of Africa's total GDP by 2015.

However, despite Nigeria's economic success in the last decade, strong economic growth wasn't followed by the required investments in its infrastructure. As such, the country's infrastructure stock has become inadequate to support its ever-increasing population and level of economic activities. At about 25% of GDP, Nigeria's stock of infrastructure is significantly lower than the global average, estimated at about 70%. As worrisome as the country's infrastructure bottlenecks were in the 50 years following its independence, they seem to have become worse, and Nigeria urgently needs to improve its outdated infrastructure.

Nigeria's underinvestment in infrastructure, historically estimated at 1.5% of GDP, contributed to its increasing challenges. This is about one-fifth of the investment level needed to keep economic growth at a minimum of 7%. To put this in perspective, countries like China and India invested 8.6% and 5% of their GDP, respectively, in infrastructure between 1992 and 2013 and this has impacted infrastructure development. For example, comparing the length of paved roads in these countries reveals India is ahead with 4,109,593 km, followed by China at 3,806,800 km and Nigeria at 200,000 km. In 2016's World Economic Forum rankings on overall infrastructure quality, Nigeria is near the bottom at 132 out of 138 countries surveyed, and well below four of the five largest economies in Africa: Morocco at 58, South Africa at 64, Egypt at 96, and Algeria at 100.

In order to effectively address Nigeria's infrastructure challenges, the country need to transition from a consumption-led growth model to an investment-led growth model, as to promote accelerated investments in infrastructure.

Rapidly growing population and urbanization in Nigeria has led to the demand for more infrastructure; in the past decade, such demands outpaced supply. New strategies need to be proffered to bring Nigeria's infrastructure stock from the current level of 25% of GDP to about 60% of GDP, which is more than double its current level of investment in infrastructure.

In 2015, Nigeria's National Planning Commission (NPC) estimated that a total of about 3 trillion dollars will be required over the next 30 years, translating to about 1 trillion dollars per decade, in order to develop and maintain the country's infrastructure. However, with dwindling revenues, occasioned by the steady decline in the price of crude oil (Nigeria's major revenue earner), it is doubtful whether it can raise such a colossal amount of money for its infrastructure development. It is therefore imperative to consider strategies to overcome the challenges.

The following strategies are recommended to drive infrastructure development in Nigeria:

Adoption of Pragmatic, visionary, and transformational leadership

Increasing Nigeria's infrastructure investments to 60% of its GDP requires a strategic move anchored on pragmatic, visionary, and transformational leadership. Pragmatic leadership is result-oriented, and it involves placing emphasis on practical issues to accomplish set goals. A pragmatic leader exhibits charisma and other attributes of visionary leadership, such as open-mindedness, foresight, sensitivity to the needs and aspirations of citizens, the capacity to predict the future, persistence, creativity, and strong conviction. As discussed in Chapter 2, these are all elements of transformational leadership.

According to Bass (1990), transformational leadership assumes that leaders with certain qualities, such as confidence, vision, and clearly stated values, are best able to motivate followers. Essentially, transformational leadership describes how leaders can initiate, develop, and implement major changes in governments and institutions. Employing the attributes of transformational leadership such as increased awareness of the importance of the task ahead, signifying the need for great vision and teamwork, emphasizing higher order needs, Nigerian leaders should be able to prioritize the task of closing the infrastructure gap in Nigeria, which is needed to lead and mobilize citizens towards massive infrastructure development, that would lead to a positive change in the narrative in infrastructure development in Nigeria. Such a pragmatic, visionary, and transformational leader will inevitably have the political will to make the necessary investments to embark on massive infrastructure development in Nigeria and bring about national development and economic prosperity.

Development planning and investment-led growth model

In the years following the attainment of independence in 1960, development planning was accepted in Nigeria as an appropriate strategy to address infrastructure needs. From 1962 to 1968, the first National Development Plan ensured that there was appreciable development of key infrastructure in different sectors of the Nigerian economy. This national development planning era was matched with discipline that ensured that about 75% of Nigeria's earned revenue was devoted to capital expenditure, leaving about 25% to recurrent expenditure. This led to enhanced infrastructure development and economic growth.

Following the abandonment of development planning during the military era, and its replacement with rolling plans from 1985 to 1999, Nigeria lost focus in its drive towards infrastructure development and economic growth. The lack of focus and continuity in the era of the rolling plans contributed immensely to the current dearth of requisite infrastructure that could propel economic growth in the country.

Good planning, consistency, commitment, and continuity of agreed-upon plans at the various stages is necessary for success and attainment of the goals and objectives of any national development plan, like the Indian example has shown. India adopted the strategy of national development planning in 1960 (the same year Nigeria adopted development planning) and has continued this approach ever since in a consistent and committed manner, implementing a total of 12 five-year development plans, spanning an uninterrupted period of 60 years. This consistency has led to high confidence in local and foreign investors in the Indian economy, which consequently attracted public-private partnership investments of about 480 billion dollars in the 12th plan (2011–2015) alone.

A return to the concept of national development planning and investment-led economic growth model in Nigeria is advocated, if the country is intent on increasing its infrastructure stock and catalyzing economic development. Beyond the return to development planning, a concerted effort should be made to ensure discipline, commitment, consistency, and continuity in the development of infrastructure contained in development plans. Effective budgeting that is well aligned to key infrastructure projects in the development plans, incremental funding of infrastructure projects, and continuity of major ongoing infrastructure projects, coupled with good governance, will be required for success.

Good governance and strengthening of institutions

In Chapter 2, it was pointed out that good governance ensures that the needs of citizens are served efficiently, effectively, and fairly. Public governance in Nigeria should aim at bringing about the best possible benefits to citizens, including the development of needed infrastructure. Governance is good when it allocates and manages resources to respond to collective socio-economic and political problems. Political leaders and bureaucrats engaged in public governance should employ good governance to provide the requisite tools for reducing poverty, deprivation, and corruption through the development of infrastructure and the efficient delivery of services to the people.

In public sector governance, institutions are central to the development process. The economic and socio-political development of most countries is dependent on their public institutions. In the past decades, weak public institutions and poor governance have been responsible for the lack of good infrastructure development in Nigeria, which has served as a trigger for poverty and corruption. However, within established accountability frameworks in democratic governance, infrastructure development can be enhanced when appropriate institutions are created and strengthened to drive infrastructure development on a sustainable basis. Furthermore, adherence to governance mechanisms that incorporate processes and guidelines that support projects to meet national goals and objectives, coupled with good project management, will ensure the successful delivery of infrastructure projects.

Rethinking National Budgetary Framework

Current budgetary practices in Nigeria can neither deliver the infrastructure needed for economic growth nor close the huge infrastructure gap in the country. In order to understand the philosophy behind Nigeria's yearly national budgets, it is necessary to interrogate the existing budgetary framework. Currently, the yearly budget is presented with pomp and pageantry by the president to the National Assembly (legislature). Promises are made by the president to develop infrastructure that will lead to economic growth and job creation; however, at the end of the budgetary year, late approval of budgets, distortion of the budget by the legislature by the time it is approved, insufficient funding, procurement problems, non-release of funds, and challenges of projects execution are advanced as reasons for the non-performance of the yearly budgets.

A cursory look at Table 6.3 for example, would reveal that from 2012 to 2015, the national budgets of Nigeria under the First National Implementation Plan of the Vision 20:2020 have been heavily tilted in favor of recurrent expenditure at an average recurrent/capital ratio of 60:40. No nation can develop the infrastructure required for growth in an economy with such paltry sums allocated to capital expenditure. Comparing the national budgets of Nigeria from 2000 to 2015 with its budgets during the first National Development Plan from 1962 to 1968 shows that the latter budgetary structure is better aligned with the goals and objectives of developing critical national infrastructure, with an average of 78% devoted to capital expenditure and recurrent expenditure averaging about 22%.

As a strategy for future development of infrastructure in Nigeria, there should be a concerted effort to prune down recurrent expenditure. Eliminating proliferation of government-owned parastatals and agencies with similar mandates will prevent the duplication of responsibilities, which often leads to needless increase in recurrent expenditure. This could have the positive effect of bringing recurrent expenditure to a maximum of about 30%, while capital expenditure could be ramped up to about 70%. This would signal seriousness on the part of the Nigerian government to address the perennial lack of infrastructure in the country by pursuing the development of new infrastructure required to drive growth in the nation's economy, create jobs, and make the delivery of services by the government more efficient and effective.

Adequate funding

In times past, misalignment between budgeting and development plans, as well as poor funding of infrastructure projects, resulted in the abandonment of key infrastructure projects in Nigeria. Adequate planning that ensures that yearly budgets are directed to development plans, coupled with adequate financing and continuity, are good strategies for success in the development of infrastructure. Effective budgeting would ensure that a substantial percentage of revenue generated from oil export is devoted to funding infrastructure development. The government could also tap into private sector resources and funding from multilateral agencies to build vital national infrastructure.

In order to ensure adequate funding for infrastructure projects, the government should look beyond its lean budgetary resources and explore creative ways of tapping into private sector finances. This can be accomplished through such mechanisms as floating infrastructure bonds for projects that are self-sustaining and therefore can be paid off over a period of time. Different private finance initiatives can also be explored to minimize funding constraints. Critical and urgent projects require adequate and timely funding that guarantees expeditious completion of the projects. Where possible, special intervention funds, infrastructure bonds, and bilateral and multilateral concessionary loans should be accessed to provide more reliable funding for critical national priority projects.

Political Stability

Political instability and insecurity over the years have negatively impacted infrastructure development in Nigeria. Foreign investors have been reluctant to provide funds for infrastructure development because of political instability. Political stability, heralding consistency, commitment, and continuity, could encourage private sector investors to invest in infrastructure development in public-private partnerships. Frequent changes in government come with policy reversals and, sometimes, abandonment of contractual obligations, creating disincentives for future investments. A climate of political instability could mean the inability of the government to focus on infrastructure development. For example, between 2012 and 2014, because of the security challenges and general insecurity, most of the government's budgeted funds went to security and defense rather than infrastructure development (see Table 8.1).

For over three decades, Nigeria has been experiencing political upheavals and frequent military take-overs. Critical infrastructure development, such as the Ajaokuta Steel Complex, Mambilla hydro-power project, and Lagos metroline project, all suffered abandonment or cancellation due to the military take-over in 1983. Such events do not lead to the creation of an enabling environment where infrastructure development can thrive. An unstable environment encourages capital flight of private sector funds that

Table 8.1 2012 FGN budget, showing huge allocation to security

Summary of 2012 FGN budget			
MDA	*Total recurrent*	*Capital*	*Total allocation*
Total budget	2.472 trillion	1.32 trillion	4,749 trillion
Statutory transfers	398,000,000,000		398,000,000,000
Ministries, departments, & agencies (MDAs)			*(In billion)*
Agriculture & rural development			78.98
Water resources			39.00
Security			921.91
Education			400.15
Federal capital territory administration			45.59
Health			282.77
Communication technology			18.31
Power			161.42
Science and technology			30.84
Transport			54.80
Petroleum resources			59.66
Works			180.80
Niger delta			59.70
Aviation			49.23
Land and housing			24.90
Total for other sectors			2,428.90

Source: National Bureau of Statistics.

could have been invested in critical infrastructure development, resulting in a positive impact on economic growth. The government could engage critical stakeholders to address the issues of political instability and insecurity, which could pave the way for increased private sector investments in infrastructure development in Nigeria.

Attracting Private Investments

The era of the first, second, third, and fourth national development plans in Nigeria saw public infrastructure delivered mainly by the public sector, by means of the traditional design-bid-construct procurement system. Public resources are unable to match the ever-increasing demands for the development of new infrastructure, and sometimes, the maintenance of old and dilapidating infrastructure. Private investments should be attracted in the development of infrastructure in the country. Public-private-partnerships (PPPs) provide an alternative system for financing infrastructure projects. PPPs are fast becoming the preferred means by which governments all over the world embark on infrastructure projects, combining the efficiency of the private sector with the service delivery of the public sector to satisfy citizens and drive economic growth and development.

The private sector can often fund projects from a large pool of resources inaccessible to governments. Consequently, in recent times, there has been a marked increase in cooperation and collaboration between the public and private sectors in order to develop and operate projects in different sectors of the economy. A public works financing database of worldwide projects between 1985 and 2004 indicates that 1,121 PPP infrastructure projects (road, rail, airport, seaport, water, and buildings), amounting to $4,509 billion worth of investments, were funded and completed, with many of these spread across Europe, Asia, and the far East.

Apart from bridging the funding gap in project delivery and operations, governments all over the world now recognize that collaboration between the public and private sectors is vital to securing dependable and sustainable funding for capital projects and reducing the pressure on fiscal budgets. In addition, public-private-partnerships offer better risk allocation between public and private sectors, and better and sustainable incentives to perform, as well as better accountability in fund utilization. It could also lead to the generation of additional revenue and an increase in the overall value of money for the national economy.

Public private partnerships in the infrastructure development in Nigeria is still at its infancy. Nigerian government should leverage on PPPs to develop critical national infrastructure, as to deliver good governance to citizens and enhance economic growth and development. To succeed with this mode of delivering new infrastructure, bureaucrats saddled with the responsibility for delivering public-private partnership infrastructure projects should take note of the critical success factors (CSFs) at the program level, which include:

- Appropriate risk allocation between public and private partners
- Transparent procurement systems
- Good governance
- Political support
- Sound economic and monetary policies, and
- Well-organized public agencies

At the implementation level, bureaucrats should understand the following important principles for success:

- Availability of public-private partnership institutional and legal framework
- Availability of public-private partnership policy and implementation units
- Perception of private finance objectives
- Perception of risk allocation and contractor compensation
- Perception of value-for-money
- Public-private partnership process transparency and disclosure
- Standardization of public-private partnership procedures and contracts, and
- Performance specifications and method specifications

In addition to these factors, strong political/leadership support is needed for success.

Manpower and material requirements

In the past, a dearth of skilled workers in public service and private engineering and construction companies led to poor service delivery in the infrastructure sector in Nigeria. With enhanced education, skill acquisition, and training, Nigeria's huge population of about 185 million can provide the necessary manpower and market to engage in the delivery of infrastructure projects. With public-private partnership infrastructure projects, new skills and competencies are required to ensure the successful delivery of infrastructure projects under the public-private partnership's framework.

A public-private-partnership-knowledgeable core staff needs to be trained and deployed in different departments of government, and charged with responsibility for policy development, dissemination of public-private partnership knowledge, and implementation of infrastructure development projects. In this way, these professionals can help to ensure that the public interest is served by the delivery of services under the public-private partnership paradigm. Increased visibility of public-private partnership advocates will foster increased collaboration between the public and private sectors in infrastructure projects, such as tolled roads, private ports, private electricity companies, private transportation companies, and private water distribution companies.

In Nigeria, most of the material resources needed for infrastructure development are imported, including bitumen for highway construction and iron and steel for bridges, railroads, and housing projects. A major reform of the infrastructure sector that could leverage on the use of locally available construction materials and manpower is vital to attract private sector investments. This is especially relevant to opening the solid minerals sector, where there is an abundance of minerals and other raw materials available for exploitation and use in the construction industry. Minerals like granite, used as aggregates in road construction and in the construction of buildings and rail tracks, abound locally. Bitumen that is used in road construction is widely available in Nigeria but largely un-exploited for infrastructure development. Similarly, limestone and iron-ore, which are used in cement manufacturing and steel bars used for reinforcement in major civil engineering constructions, such as bridges, buildings, culverts, jetties, and other engineering projects, abound in various parts of the country. These materials should be exploited in a way that would create new value-chains in the building and construction industry and thereby stemming the tide of capital flight abroad in the importation of these materials. In this vein therefore, the government should as a matter of priority, takes steps to resume completion works in the various steel rolling mills, and Ajaokuta Steel Complex, which was abandoned at about 90 percent completion, over three decades ago.

The government should establish a deliberate policy regarding the use of local construction materials to stimulate value-addition in the solid minerals sector and bring about job creation, which has the potential to solve the high unemployment levels in Nigeria. This will inevitably contribute to economic growth. Local sourcing of materials and requisite manpower could be integrated into the design and specifications of infrastructure projects in Nigeria to eliminate the need for imported construction materials and manpower, thereby minimizing the costs of infrastructure projects.

The government could also patronize local construction companies and help them in building business capacities and capabilities that would enable them to carry out most of the infrastructure projects in Nigeria and, by so doing, check the menace of capital flight occasioned by the wholesale patronage of foreign engineering and construction companies. In addition to creating a vast new value chain in the construction industry in Nigeria, patronizing local construction materials and companies will help to improve the technical, industrial, supervisory, and managerial skills and competencies that will be required in the construction industry to meet new challenges. This could ultimately lead to the gainful employment of millions of Nigerians.

Monitoring and evaluation of infrastructure projects

Monitoring and evaluation is an essential component of project management, especially during the implementation stage. Its presence or absence can be the difference between the success or failure of development policies, programs, and projects. As an authentic tool for measuring inputs; outputs; outcomes; and the impact of policies, programs, and projects on the economy, there should be clearly established goals and targets, including key performance indicators, against which performance could be measured and assessed.

A monitoring and evaluation framework has an inherent feedback mechanism that helps to correct any policy or plan errors, ensuring that their goals and objectives are well served. It is good practice to compile and circulate monthly or quarterly reports from the field in order to assist policy makers in making judgments about whether to alter any aspect of the plan when things are not going well or to reinforce the plan when things are going as expected. Good monitoring and evaluation frameworks are required for the success of development plans at the implementation stage. The lofty goals and objectives of development and strategic plans cannot be realized in the absence of an effective monitoring and evaluation mechanism, backed by the necessary political will, resources, commitment, consistency, and continuity.

Combating corruption

It is a commonly held opinion in Nigeria that most government officials at all levels have vested interests in the award of contracts that adversely affect their performance in the infrastructure sector. According to Transparency International (2013), the infrastructure sector in Nigeria is associated with corruption. Estimates of financial losses range between 10% and 30% of the total value of publicly funded construction projects. The failure of most of the country's infrastructure projects could be due to corruption among bureaucrats.

Analysis of project failure in Nigeria identified bureaucratic corruption, lack of professionalism, inexperienced project managers and project personnel, and non-transparent procurement processes as the main causes of project failure. Even when transparent processes guide the awarding of contracts for infrastructure projects, such as in public-private partnership infrastructure projects and the Public Procurement Act, corruption may still rear its head at the implementation stage.

Bureaucrats saddled with the responsibility of ensuring that the project's technical specifications and budget are met could be compromised and sometimes collude with contractors to undermine the government and public interest. A good strategy to mitigate this is to ensure that corrupt practices are tamed through ensuring that the bureaucratic institutions involved in infrastructure development are made more transparent and accountable. Punitive actions should be enforced against erring project personnel who engage in corrupt and unethical practices to serve as a deterrent to others. Governance mechanisms that integrate transparent processes and guidelines that assist projects in meeting organizational objectives should be put in place to avoid project failure.

Summary

Having reviewed the barriers to infrastructure development in Chapter 7, the focus of Chapter 8 has been on considering strategies to overcome the barriers. Some of the approaches considered included the need to establish pragmatic, visionary, and transformational leadership, along with planning and good governance. Proposed strategies to address the funding requirements included restructuring budgets and ensuring that adequate funds are directed toward infrastructure projects and not diverted. Finally, it was pointed out that political stability and public-private-partnerships are key to building new infrastructures, maintaining and repairing existing ones, and monitoring all activities to counter corruption and ensure progress. In Chapter 9, we turn our attention to what has been achieved and what is possible.

Bibliography

Akinwale, A. A. (2010). The menace of inadequate infrastructure in Nigeria. *African Journal of Science, Technology, Innovation and Development,* 2(3), 207–228. Retrieved from www.ajstid.com

Anigbogu, N. A., & Shwarka, M. S. (2011). Evaluation of the impact of the public procurement reform program on combating corrupt practices in public building projects delivery in Nigeria. *Environtech Journal,* 1(2), 43–51. Retrieved from www.google.com

Babatunde, S. O., Opawole, A., & Akinsiku, O. E. (2012). Critical success factors in public-private partnership (PPP) on infrastructure delivery in Nigeria. *Journal of Facilities Management,* 10(3), 212–225. doi:10.1108/14725961211246018. Can't access.

Cheema, G. S. (2005). *Building democratic institutions: Governance reform in developing countries.* New York, NY: Kumarian Press.

Craven, J. (2017). *The importance of infrastructure.* Retrieved from www.thoughtco.com/what-is-infrastructure-why-important-1777

Dahiru, D., Abdul Azeez, A. D., & Bala, K. (2013). *Study of measures for enhancing public-private partnership towards infrastructure development in Nigeria.* Conference Paper on Sustainable Building. Coventry University. Retrieved from www.coventry.ac.uk/Global/Faculty%20events/SB13/SB13–42-Study-of-measures-for-enhancing-public-private-partnership-towards-infrastructural-development-in-Nigeria.pdf

Ekpenkhio, S. A. (2003). Public sector procurement reforms: The Nigerian experience. Conference Paper. Nigeria. Retrieved from www.wto.org

Ezeh, E. M. (2013). *Public procurement reform strategies*. Retrieved from https://cips.org/Documents/Engr.%20Emeka%20Ezeh%20presentation%20%2821%20May%29%20%5BRepaired%5D.pdf

Gwilliam, K. (2011). *Africa's transport infrastructure: Mainstreaming maintenance and management*. Washington, DC: The World Bank.

Idris, A., Kura, S. M., & Bashir, M. U. (2013). Public private partnership in Nigeria and improvement in service delivery: An appraisal. *Journal of Humanities and Social Sciences, 10*(3), 63–71. Retrieved from www.Iosrjournals.org

Kemp, R., Parto, S., & Gibson, R. B. (2005). Governance for sustainable development: Moving from theory to practice. *International Journal of Sustainable Development, 8*(1/2), 12–30. doi:10.1504/IJSD.2005.007372

Lawal, T., & Oluwatoyin, A. (2011). National development in Nigeria: Issues, challenges and prospects. *Journal of Public Administration and Policy Research, 3*(9), 237–241. doi:10.5897/JPAR11.012

Marcellus, I. C. (2009). Development planning in Nigeria: Reflections on the national economic empowerment and development strategies (NEEDS) 2003–2007. *Journal of Social Sciences, 20*(30), 197–210.

Mbanefo, C. A. (2000). The role of engineering infrastructure in national development. In M. D. Abdullahi (Ed.), *Provision & maintenance of engineering infrastructure for technological development in Nigeria* (pp. 37–44). Kaduna: Fahimta Publishing Company.

Mohammed, K., Chapola, D., & Bello, A. (2013). The state of Nigerian economy in the 21st century: Privatization and commercialization programs under Obasanjo-Atiku regime. *European Scientific Journal, 9*(19), 88–98. Retrieved from http://eujournal.org/index.php/esj/

Muogbo, S. U. (2013). Impact of privatization on corporate performance: A study of selected industries in Nigeria. *International Journal of Humanities and Social Science Invention, 2*(7), 81–89. ISSN (Online): 2319–7722. Retrieved from www.ijhssi.org/papers/v2%287%29/Version-1/K0271081089.pdf

Mustafa, A. R. (2006). Ethnic structure, inequality and governance of the public sector in Nigeria. *United Nations Research Institute for Social Development*, 1–55. Retrieved from www.unrisd.org

Ngowi, H. P. (2009). Economic development and change in Tanzania since independence: The political leadership factor. *African Journal of Political Science and International Relations, 3*(4), 259–267. Retrieved from www.academicjournals.org/ajpsir/index.htm

Nwanolue, B. O. G., & Iwuoha, V. C. (2012). The Nigerian civil service and promotion of sustainable human development: A critical analysis. *Arabian Journal of Business and Management Review, 1*(9), 12–21. Retrieved from www.arabianjbmr.com

Nzongola-Ntalaja, G. (2002). *UNDP role in promoting good governance*. Seminar for the International Guest at the Congress of the Labor Party, Oslo, Norway. Retrieved from www.um.edu.mt/_data/assets/pdf_file/0003/120837/2009_4.pdf

Ogbonna, A. C. & Kalu, L. U. (2012). Public procurement reform in developing countries: A critique of the real estate context in the Nigerian case. *International Journal of Management Sciences and Business Research, 1*(8), 65–77. Retrieved from www.ijmsbr.com/

Rotberg, R. I. (2005). Strengthening governance: Ranking countries would help. *The Washington Quarterly, 28*(1), 71–81. doi:10.1162/0163660042518215

Shafritz, J. M., Russell, E. W., & Boricks, C. P. (2007). *Introducing public administration* (5th ed.). New York, NY: Pearson Longman.

Taye, O. O., & Dada, M. O. (2012). Appraisal of private sector involvement in infrastructure development in Lagos, Nigeria. *Mediterranean Journal of Social Sciences, 3*(2), 399–412. doi:10.5901/mjss.2012.v3n2.399

Udoka, C. A., & Anyingang, R. A. (2012). The effects of privatization on economic growth on Nigeria: 1979–2007 in retrospect. *International Journal of Economic Development, Research and Investment, 3*(2), 25–35. Retrieved from www.icidr.org/

UNDP. (1997). Reconceptualizing governance. Discussion paper 2, Management Development and Governance.

United Nations. (2007). *Public governance indicators: A literature review.* Retrieved from http://unpan1.un.org

9 The importance of infrastructure development

Infrastructure is the bedrock of a society's development. It contributes immensely to the economic development of any nation by increasing productivity and providing amenities that enhance its people's quality of life. A solid and adequate infrastructure base will translate into an increased aggregate output and a flourishing economy. African countries, including Nigeria, face challenges in providing and maintaining such infrastructure as roads, railways, airports and seaports, telecommunications, power plants and electricity, portable water, and housing. Roads constitute a major infrastructure in any developing nation, and dominate the transport sector in Africa. In Nigeria, highways and rural roads make up the essential network of transportation on which economic prosperity hinges. While the railway system is relatively underdeveloped, air transportation caters to less than 1% of the population.

Following independence in 1960, Nigeria inherited limited infrastructure from colonial Britain, including tarred roads of minimal dimension, railways, ports, urban electricity, health centers, schools, basic communication networks, etc. Nigeria is replete with examples of inadequate infrastructure, including the irregular supply of electricity, shortage of portable water, fuel scarcity, unreliable health care services, poor educational facilities, bad roads, malfunctioning ports, and erratic telecommunication services. Compared to other countries in Asia, Nigeria is significantly slower in the pace of infrastructure development. There is need for urgent measures to address this infrastructure deficiency (Adeyeri, 2013). Nigeria's socio-economic transformation depends on a strong infrastructure base. How can Nigeria improve investment in its infrastructure?

Around the world, investment in infrastructure has always played a leading role in economic development. Basic infrastructure such as roads, railways, airports, electricity (power) generation and supply, water supply, and sanitation underpins sustainable development and the economic transformation of emerging economies. Infrastructure investment is needed in Nigeria to expand transport systems, power generation, supply and transmission, water collection and supply, sanitation systems, and communications systems (telecommunications, Internet, etc.). Such investments will lead to rapid economic and social development.

There is uncontroverted evidence that investment in infrastructure leads to the growth of a country's economy and the improved well-being of its people. According to the McKinsey Global Institute (2015), over the next two decades, the world would need to invest $57 trillion on infrastructure to realize global economic growth ambitions. In the UK alone, infrastructure spending may need to run at about £50 billion per year until 2030 to meet demand. In Nigeria, $3 trillion is the estimated investment for infrastructure development in the next 30 years to ensure maximization of economic and social growth (National Planning Commission, 2014). The McKinsey Global Institute pointed out that much of that investment should go to electricity (power), transportation, and real estate. This would mean annual infrastructure investments of more than $50 billion to propel economic and social growth. However, with dwindling oil prices and a fall in the country's GDP's growth rate, which stood at 6.5% in 2014, it is doubtful that Nigeria will be able to raise such colossal sums of money for investment in infrastructure. As a country, Nigeria needs to move away from its consumption-led growth model to an investment-led growth model, which would support enhanced investments in infrastructure.

With increasing budget deficits and high borrowing costs, the government seems to have lost substantial ground in its efforts to boost infrastructure investment. Despite current efforts by the Nigerian government to invest in infrastructure with record budget appropriations for capital expenditures, it is obvious that the required level of improvement will necessitate not only increased public investment but also the promotion of a more friendly environment for private investment.

Under the public-private partnership scheme, Nigeria could attain infrastructure sufficiency in the following sectors: education, health, housing, information and communication technology (ICT), transportation, and power. To attract investors in these sectors and achieve the level of investments required to transform Nigeria's infrastructure, the government will be required to diligently execute target infrastructure plans. A robust framework for private investments will ultimately lead to the availability of private funding, thereby ensuring the protection of future private investments in infrastructure.

Infrastructure development and socio-economic growth

Infrastructure development has led to socio-economic growth in Nigeria, which, in turn, has impacted its citizens' standard of living. Infrastructure facilitates the production of goods and services. For example, good road infrastructure facilitates the supply of raw materials from farms and mines to markets and factories, and distribution of finished products to end-users. Evidence abounds from the past, when good infrastructure development led to a general improvement in the standard of living of the people through the enhancement of the capacity of citizens to pursue productive ventures and thus contribute to the country's GDP.

Between 1960 and 2015, through the efforts of various political leaderships and administrations, there has been significant development of infrastructure in Nigeria. At this juncture, let us look at how these infrastructures have impacted socio-economic growth in different sectors of the country's economy.

Transportation

At the time of the post-independent government (1960–1963) and during the first republic (1963–1966), a significant part of the public capital expenditure was devoted to investment in the transportation sector. An average of 20% of public capital expenditure was invested in transportation during the eras of the first National Development Plan (1962–1968), the second National Development Plan (1970–1974), the third National Development Plan (1975–1980), and the fourth National Development Plan (1981–1985). From 1990 to 1998, during the time of the first National Rolling Plan (1990–1993), the second National Rolling Plan (1994–1996), and the third National Rolling Plan (1996–1998), an average of 10% of planned public-sector expenditure was devoted to transportation.

In Nigeria, transportation infrastructure contributes to GDP growth, improves private sector productivity, creates jobs, and improves living standards. Studies indicate that transportation expenditure in Nigeria had a significant effect on output growth. However, its population of 185 million people means that Nigeria requires an even greater investment in transportation to reach the level of modern inter-modal transportation networks. Such networks would result in an improved method of moving citizens, goods, and services from one part of the country to another, thereby promoting trade and social integration, as well as catalyzing growth in the nation's economy.

This could lead to the massive employment of skilled and semiskilled personnel in the transportation sector, where they would become engaged in engineering and haulage and associated jobs, and help hitherto unemployed Nigerians to achieve good livelihoods. Improved roads and rail transportation infrastructure could further lead to the reduction of travel times in Nigeria, making passenger transport and haulage more affordable and profitable. Apart from the quick turn-around enabled by better roads and refurbished rail lines, the consequential reduction in vehicle maintenance because of better roads and less wear and tear would lead to more profitability for transporters and haulage companies.

Agriculture

Agriculture is the largest sector of the Nigerian economy, with GDP contribution of about 40%. Research shows that Nigeria has over 80 million hectares of arable land. This accounts for about 23% of arable land across all West Africa. The Nigerian government, under the agriculture transformation initiative (2012–2015), began to implement key reforms geared towards turning agriculture into a business that makes money, with a focus on investments as opposed to aid and development.

During those years, improving prospects for the agricultural sector were caused by a growing demand for food, driven by a large population, growing incomes, and higher prices due to demand in the international market. As a result, the federal government launched the Youth Employment in Agricultural Program (YEAP), called the "Nagropreneur" program, which was designed to encourage youths to enter the field of commercial agriculture as entrepreneurs, with a goal of having 750,000 youths in the program by 2015. Additionally, the federal government launched staple crop-processing zones to support investments in the entire agricultural value-chain. This led to significant private investment commitments from agribusiness ventures, such as the flour mills of Nigeria, the Dangote Group, and Indorama.

The federal government, through the Ministry of Agriculture, announced a supportive program with the goal of creating a Nigerian agricultural sector worth $256 billion by 2030. Using this gesture, the government stated its intention to stop food importation, valued at over ₦1 trillion annually, and ensure a massive growth in the sector, in partnership with the private sector. Set against the annual loss of funds to importation, ₦350 billion would accrue in the nation's economy by the end of 2015, following the import substitution policy for rice, while the substitution of wheat flour content in bread with cassava flour was estimated to generate over ₦60 billion. In 2012, Nigeria rolled out an ambitious reform program across its agricultural sector, aimed at cutting the country's dependency on food imports, creating jobs, and generating growth. These reforms, coupled with the move to privatize the procurement and distribution of fertilizer and seed, resulted in more private sector participation and an increase in foreign direct investments.

There is a consensus among stakeholders that the key to unlocking the growth potential of agriculture in Nigeria is to improve the lot of small-scale farmers. The federal government empowered millions of small holder farmers under the agricultural transformation initiative (2012–2015). These farmers had access to millions of hectares through loans from the central bank of Nigeria's dedicated agriculture fund, provided to ensure they have access to appropriate inputs and financing that will significantly boost productivity under the Agricultural Franchise Model. This will make the small-holder farmer a franchisee of a larger farm, with access to all the necessary inputs.

This model minimized the risks associated with investing in the sector and has thereby stimulated the financial sector to invest in the agricultural sector. These positive initiatives in agriculture, coupled with the provision of transportation infrastructure (roads, rail, and water), telecommunication infrastructure, and irrigation, combined to produce increased agricultural productivity, leading to economic growth. Modern telecommunication infrastructure enabled mobile telephony and made it possible for the Nigerian government to engage private sector participants in the procurement and distribution of seeds and fertilizers. The mobile telephony made it possible to create an audit tray that improved transparency and accountability in the distribution of fertilizers, farm inputs and grants, ensuring a good nation-wide penetration of over ten million farmers. This led to savings of about 25 billion naira annually, in contrast to the 40 years (1970–2010) for which government directly procured and distributed fertilizers and seeds to farmers through its agencies.

In addition, the provision of extensive irrigation infrastructure made possible dry season rice farming in the ten northern states of Bauchi, Gombe, Jigawa, Kano, Katsina, Kebbi, Kogi, Niger, Sokoto, and Zamfara. This led to the employment of about 300,000 farmers and production of an average of one million metric tons of rice. In the rice value-chain alone, in 2011, only about 400 thousand farmers were reached, and 20,000 metric tons of seeds and 50,000 metric tons of fertilizers were distributed by the government. By 2014, aided by the new telecommunication infrastructure, about six million farmers were reached, and 100,000 metric tons of seeds and 650,000 metric tons of fertilizers were distributed through the participation of private sector players.

The construction of rural-urban roads provided good access to the markets from the farms, leading to the early transportation of farm produce to the markets. This translated into good income for the farmers, who had previously suffered losses due to their inaccessibility of the market and when farm produce was stranded. This, in turn, led to appreciable socioeconomic growth, with the agricultural sector contributing about 40% of the country's GDP.

The social-economic growth impact includes the creation of about two million jobs; production of seven million metric tons of rice paddy by six million farmers, with a net value addition of 400 billion naira to the country's GDP; and decrease in the cost of a bag of rice from N14,500.00 in 2012 to N8,000.00 by 2014. This not only led to a reduction in the national supply gap of this most sought-after Nigerian staple, from 2.6 million metric tons in 2011 to 1.5 million metric tons in 2014, but also rice became more affordable for all income brackets in Nigeria.

Education

In the education sector, development of needed infrastructure led to a marked improvement in school enrolment in parts of the country. In the north, the development of special schools for *almajiris* (street urchins) not only led to the removal of thousands of children from the streets in the northern states of Kaduna, Kebbi, Jigawa, Kaduna, Kano, Zamfara, and Sokoto but enhanced enrolment in schools. Attending school will help these children to be educated and equipped with skills they will use throughout their lives.

Information and communication technology (ICT)

With a growth rate of 32.5% and GDP contribution of 7%, Nigeria has established itself as the largest telecommunication market in Africa. The country's telecom sector is undergoing speedy transformation because of explosive growth and rapid infrastructure development. Liberalization of the telecom sector and increased competition among players have brought substantial benefits to the consumers in terms of lower subscription rates and enhanced choices, leading to socio-economic growth. The introduction of mobile number portability (MNP), along with the issuance of 3G and 4G licenses, is already playing a significant role in driving growth in the telecom sector in the country. Nigeria's mobile market possesses tremendous growth potential, given the fact that the penetration rate is over 60%. With rapidly improving mobile infrastructure and intense competition among mobile operators, it is expected that the number of mobile subscribers will grow at a compound annual growth rate (CAGR) of around 15% over the next five years, with a penetration rate exceeding 90% by the end of 2018.

Communication infrastructure provided by the government and private sector partners has ensured that about 93.5 million Nigerians have active access to the Internet. This has enabled the population to create wealth and value through online and digital platforms, providing them with opportunities to earn a decent living. These free online platforms offer tech-savvy Nigerians the opportunity to acquire new customers for their business, provide excellent customer services, improve their employees' productivity, hire and train employees, improve sales, and develop marketing and advertising, leading to increased revenue and profits.

Housing supply

Under the first national implementation plan of vision 20:2020, over 61,000 housing units were constructed, providing affordable and decent accommodation to over 300,000 Nigerians across the six geo-political zones in the country. This led to better environmental health and the improved well-being of families living in these housing units. Following private investments in the housing sector, about 500,000 additional housing apartments have been added to the housing stock by 2015, leading to better and cheaper housing units, with enhanced sanitation and hygiene.

Health

Primary health care initiatives launched by successive governments since independence have resulted in the development of primary health care centers in about 7,740 wards and general hospitals in 774 local government areas. In addition, many specialists and teaching hospitals in the 36 states of the federation have been able to handle primary, secondary and tertiary health care delivery in the country, and the provision of health infrastructure under the "Save one million lives" program, involved the scaling up of six cost-effective interventions. These interventions include maternal and child health, nutrition, prevention of mother to child transmission of HIV, provision of essential commodities, malaria control, routine immunization and eradication of polio, leading to the saving of about 450,000 lives.

Manufacturing

The performance of the Nigerian manufacturing sector has been poor in recent years, as it has been contributing only 5% to the nation's GDP. According to the West African Institute of Financial and Economic Management, in developed countries where the manufacturing sector is thriving, manufacturing contributes as much as 35%–40% to the GDP. For instance, in Malaysia, the manufacturing sector contributes about 45%. Herein lies the root of the unemployment and low level of productivity in Nigeria. Unless the comatose manufacturing sector is revitalized and made to contribute between 35% and 40% to the country's GDP, the Nigerian economy will continue to be consumption-driven, with negative consequences for its citizens.

Political and economic factors have contributed greatly to the decline of the Nigerian manufacturing sector. For instance, poor infrastructure and epileptic electricity power supply are key impediments to this sector, and lately, lack of access to foreign exchange for limited raw materials, engineering tools, and equipment are also inimical to its performance. The sector operates on more than 70% of the electricity power it generates from individual generators. Huge running costs do not make their products competitive in the market as operating these generators greatly increase the cost of manufacturing goods. The government should take steps to improve electricity generation, transmission and distribution to mitigate the high cost of running generators and improve manufacturing activities in the country.

In order to ramp up manufacturing in Nigeria, the political leaders should formulate policies that will prohibit export of raw materials in their crude form, and mandate exporters of raw materials, to ensure that purposeful processing of raw materials are first carried out, to add value to the raw materials before exporting same. In the process of adding value to raw materials, jobs would be created and will lead to employment of many Nigerians, and stem rural-urban migration in the country.

Electricity (power) supply

In Nigeria, electricity (power) is one of the major forms of energy needed for production services. It is not only a highly demanded resource but a tool for good living. It is a vital infrastructural component of economic growth. In all economies, households and businesses, especially factories, have extensive demand for electricity. This demand is driven by several key factors, such as industrialization, extensive urbanization, population growth, and rising standard of living. However, the electricity subsector in Nigeria has been plagued by many challenges, such as inadequate capacity, poor power generation, power loss in transmission, and inadequate maintenance. These, among other constraining factors, have kept the electricity supply in Nigeria below the national demand.

This imbalance between supply and demand in the power sector in Nigeria has lingered since the first republic after independence in 1960. Successive leaderships and administrations have made efforts to meet the demand for electricity power, leading to increments in installed capacity from 804 MW/h in 1970 to 2330.5 MW/h in 1980. In 2010, the federal government launched the power reform plan, which saw the unbundling of the power holding company (PHCN) into six generation companies and 11 distribution companies in an unprecedented privatization move to improve the electricity supply in Nigeria and thereby drive economic growth. In 2014, installed capacity was raised to 12,323 MW/h, the highest level attained in the history of the power sector in Nigeria. However, the country's demand for electricity continues to increase with increases in population and urbanization. The inability of electricity supply to meet demand has led to some negative impacts on productivity.

The ubiquitous role of electricity in daily economic and social activities has compelled many households and business organizations to acquire electrical power generating sets to either supplement or complement the public supply of electricity. This has resulted in additional economic costs, such as the cost of production for business organizations. Also, carbon monoxide emitted by the power generating sets pollute the environment and impairs good health. To check the high production costs, many business organizations are forced to operate below capacity, which results in low productivity and a stunted GDP growth. Although the federal government entered various memoranda of understanding (MoU) with worldwide leaders in the power sector, including General Electric (GE) of the United States, Siemens of Germany, Eletrobras of Brazil, and the Power-Water Construction Corporation (PCC) of China, for the development of 20,000 MW gas power and 10,000 kilometers of transmission line, the gains of these and other initiates are yet to be realized as the projects have not been fully implemented. As such, these initiatives have not resulted in additional megawatts of electricity in Nigeria.

Nigeria is a highly energy-dependent country, and electricity is in high demand, not only for production activities but in daily activities. Nigeria cannot experience exponential growth in its GDP until its electrical power problems are solved, and the country's electricity supply outpaces demand. Until this situation is reached, Nigeria will not be able to create jobs to engage the huge unemployed labor force, which will lead to a loss of trust in the government by citizens.

Summary

Throughout this book, attempts have been made to explain and define infrastructure. This chapter has focused on many infrastructure sectors to discuss some specific examples of the challenges and successes they have faced. To understand the implications for the socio-economic development of Nigeria, we have examined eight sectors in particular: transportation, agriculture, education, information and communication technology, housing and water, health, manufacturing, and electrical power supply. We have shown that growth in these sectors will contribute to growth of the overall GDP and an increase in the well-being and economic stability of all Nigerians.

Bibliography

Adeyeri, S. (2013). Conflicts and political instability in Nigeria; A critical discourse. *International Journal of Advanced Research in Management and Social Sciences, 2*(10), 119–130. Retrieved from www.academia.edu

Afegbua, I. A. (2010). Conflicts and political instability in Nigeria: Causes, consequences and prospects. *Journal of Social Science and Public Policy, 2*, 10–18.

Afeikhena, J. (2002). *Public enterprises reform in Nigeria: Evidence from the telecommunications industry*. Nairobi: African Economic Research Consortium.

Africa, G. (2014). *Fertilizer subsidy reform revives Nigeria's agriculture: Case studies on public-private agriculture investments*. Retrieved from www.growafrica.com

Jonathan, G. (2015). *Innovative reforms of President Goodluck Jonathan's administration* (pp. 17–24). Abuja: The Office of the Chief Economic Adviser to the President.

Kemp, R., Parto, S., & Gibson, R. B. (2005). Governance for sustainable development: Moving from theory to practice. *International Journal of Sustainable Development, 8*(1/2), 12–30. doi:10.1504/IJSD.2005.007372

Mustafa, A. R. (2006). *Ethnic structure, inequality and governance of the public sector in Nigeria. United Nations Research Institute for Social Development*, 1–55. Retrieved from www.unrisd.org

Naswem, A. A., Okwoche, V. A., & Age, A. I. (2016). Mainstreaming sustainability in the Nigerian agricultural transformation agenda. *World*, 3(1), 054–059.

Natsa, R. (2015). *Nigeria: As FG launches ATA-SP Phase 1*. All Africa. Retrieved from http://allafrica.com/stories/201503130138.html

Ogbonna, B. C. (2012). Structural adjustment program (SAP) in Nigeria. An empirical assessment. *Journal of Banking, 6*(1), 19–40. Retrieved from www.academia.edu/

Ogu, V. I. (2000). Stakeholders' partnership approach to infrastructure provision and management in developing world cities: Lessons from the sustainable Ibadan project. *Human Settlement Development, 111*, 1–18. doi:10.1016/S0197–3975(00)00015-1

Olumide, H. A. (2011). Telecommunication reform and effects of competition on availability, quality and cost of services in Nigeria. *Public Policy and Administration Research, 1*(3), 8–20. Retrieved from www.iist.org/Journals/index.php/PPAR

10 Conclusion

Review of the chapters

The purpose of this book is to examine the status of infrastructure development in Nigeria during the 55 years after its Independence, from 1960 to 2015. In order to explore this large issue in depth, the content was broken down into chapters. We will revisit these chapters as we prepare to draw some conclusions about Nigerian infrastructure.

The first chapter of the book introduced the country that we now know as Nigeria. We learned something of its people and culture and gained insights into its landscape and traditions. We also reviewed the ways in which the nineteenth-century British government built a basic infrastructure for the purpose of bringing the landlocked natural resources of the emerging country to the coast so that they could be shipped to Great Britain. We discovered that several protectorates came together to form what we now know as Nigeria, and soon after, in 1960, the country gained independence from Britain. We saw that successive governments and leaders took control, and it became evident that there was a great need to build an infrastructure base that would allow the new country to thrive, gain economic independence, and provide a sustainable way of life for its citizens.

The scene set by the previous chapter, Chapter 2 digressed from explaining the history and geo-political nature of Nigeria into an in-depth consideration of the kind of leadership and type of governance that would best help the country build its infrastructure base. Concepts and theories about leaders and leadership styles were examined, and definitions of governance were presented. The chapter concluded that the approach described as transformational leadership might serve Nigeria well. Transformational leaders, it was suggested, have the vision, the selflessness, and the personality traits to effect change and inspire the citizenry. With this paradigm in mind, it became possible to analyze how leadership and governance affect initiatives to develop infrastructure.

Chapter 3 guided us through the governmental polices of the 55 years from 1960 to 2015, giving us an overview of the leadership during that period and pointing out the moves from democratically elected governments to military rule and back again. A summary of the major infrastructure projects taken on by each leader was provided, and we paused regularly to reflect on what kind of leadership had been displayed, drawing on the theories presented in Chapter 2. We compared and contrasted the styles of the military leaders with those of the elected presidents of the sometimes-brief republics. It was evident that some leaders were more effective than others in helping Nigeria to build its infrastructure base.

A more careful look at the reforms undertaken by the various regimes was undertaken in Chapter 4 in order to provide more information about what succeeded and what failed. Under the umbrella of economic reforms, this chapter explained privatization initiatives, reforms in the energy sector, banking and insurance, and telecommunications sectors. The human side of reform was seen in efforts to provide infrastructures that would reduce poverty, introduce changes in agriculture, and improve educational opportunities. A review of the role of the civil service showed a sharp decline in its effectiveness after the British departed, and we discussed the reasons for which bureaucracies became unproductive and even corrupt. It was not surprising to learn that infrastructure development had suffered many blows.

With things looking bleak, we moved on to Chapter 5 and the discovery that National Development Plans had helped to maintain what little infrastructure existed at independence and aided in preparing for new projects. The first four plans were crafted between 1962 and 1985, and we looked at each one, in turn, to see how its objectives and implementation had contributed to infrastructure development. We found that the fifth plan, although it was presented in 1984, was never carried out. Instead, rolling plans and a more holistic approach to planning gained favor and planted the seeds for the launching of a new vision.

Vision 20:2020 was explained in Chapter 6. It was founded with the intention to place Nigeria alongside the top 20 economies in the world by the year 2020. The vision 20:2020 policy document was launched with the First National Implementation Plan in 2012, acting on the 'Transformation Agenda' that was the framework for moving forward with this ambitious undertaking. We studied the three pillars of the vision and learned the results of a series of implementation plans. Budget forms showed how the actual funding of projects at the implementation stage fell far short of the proposed funding at the planning stage; nevertheless, some considerable success was recorded in some sectors.

But challenges need to be understood too, and that is why Chapter 7 was devoted to exploring the issue of corruption, along with other obstacles to infrastructure development. This chapter began by pointing out that Nigeria has been regarded as one of the most corrupt countries in the world. The dimensions and causes provided details of how corruption first reared its head in the country and a discussion of corruption in the civil service showed how corrupt practices spread. But corruption is not the only obstacle to progress in infrastructure development in Nigeria. Political instability, the civil war, the lack of skilled workers, and the impact of successive military rulers are just some of the issues that were presented in this chapter.

Chapter 8, though, focused on more positive issues, explaining what strategies are needed in order to make infrastructure a priority for leaders and governments. Visionary and transformational leadership were emphasized as key ingredients. Good governance, strong budgetary architecture, political stability, and provision of local building materials and manpower were all listed. The need to build public-private partnerships and the imperative to combat corruption were two strategies that were emphasized.

To emphasize the need for infrastructure development throughout the country, Chapter 9 provided an overview of projects according to sector and their impacts on socio-economic growth. Examples of growth in transportation, agriculture, education, information & communication technology (ICT), housing, health, manufacturing, and electrical power showed that there has, in fact, been considerable progress in recent years. However, the message remains that infrastructure development is foundational if Nigeria is to achieve the lofty goals it set in Vision 20:2020.

This concluding chapter allows us to review the major issues that have been discussed in the book, to make some recommendations for future initiatives, and to summarize 12 themes that have emerged from these reflections about leadership and the governance of infrastructure development in Nigeria.

Themes emerging from the examination of infrastructure development

Impact of the policies of previous military administrations

Military governance of infrastructure development in Nigeria had some benefits, particularly in the areas of highway construction, electrical power production, transportation, and construction of airports and seaports. This can be attributed to the fact that Nigeria was governed for a longer period by the military than by civilian administrations. Between 1981 and 2000, the military constructed about 14,832 km of paved roads and 27.38 km of highway bridges. Similar trends are revealed by archival data during the Gowon administration (1966–1975). Housing, power, and telecommunications recorded a considerable surge during military governance.

It can be argued that adherence to planning principles and the national development plans, coupled with earnings from the sale of crude oil, accounted more than any other factor for the success of the military administrations in infrastructure development, especially between 1966 and 1985, when Babangida took over the leadership of Nigeria. However, the military paid little attention to rural infrastructure development and the construction of railroads. Although Babangida set up the directorate for food, roads and rural infrastructure (DFRRI) during his tenure between 1985 and 1993 to mitigate the situation in rural areas, it was short-lived as it was abrogated by subsequent military regime.

The accomplishments by the military in the development of infrastructure were partly due to the remarkable increase in oil revenue during the Gowon administration (1966–1975), the Babangida administration (1985–1993), and the Abacha administration (1993–1998). Nigeria's export revenue from oil rose significantly during these political periods (Okonjo-Iweala, 2012). Money was available to fund infrastructure development.

Under a focused military dictatorship, government plans and projects are implemented faster than they are in civilian democratic systems due to the authoritarian nature of military regimes with inherent command and control. Political bickering and delays in legislative approval and bureaucratic procedures in civilian democratic administrations in Nigeria have a way of slowing down the implementation of infrastructure projects. Nigerian military leaders governed by decrees and dictatorial ordinances and paid no attention to accountability issues that usually lead to delays in project implementations in a democratic setting. Under authoritarian leadership style, decision making is faster as the leader makes decisions with little or no input from the rest of the group, unlike in the democratic leadership style, where consensus is usually developed sometimes leading to delays (Rogger, 2014).

However, within an established accountable framework in democratic governance, infrastructure governance can be enhanced, and projects can be delivered in a timely manner when appropriate institutions are created and strengthened to drive infrastructure development on sustainable basis. Adherence to governance mechanisms that incorporate processes and guidelines that support projects to meet organizational objectives coupled with good project management will ensure the timely completion of projects.

Contribution of policy formulation and implementation

The national development plan policies have been shown to contribute immensely to the development of infrastructure in Nigeria. The first national development plan (1962–1968) was formulated with the objective of creating development opportunities in transportation, hydropower, health, education, and employment. The second development plan (1970–1974) prioritized agriculture, industry, transport, manpower, defense, electricity, communication, and water supply. Notably, it was during the military administration of General Yakubu Gowon that key infrastructure development became a priority in the Nigerian national development planning scheme.

The third national development plan (1975–1980) focused mainly on rural agricultural development programs such as the operation feed the nation (OFN) and industrial development during the Obasanjo administration. The infrastructure development policies of the Gowon administration, such as the infrastructures associated with the planned festival of arts & culture (FESTAC) in 1977, were continued. Marcellus (2009) categorized national development planning in Nigeria into four phases: the colonial era (pre-1960 independence), the fixed medium-term era (1962–1985), the era of the rolling plan (1986–1998), and the new democratic dispensation era (1999 – present). It was within the era of the fixed medium-term that four successful national development plans were executed with significant impact on infrastructure development.

These milestones demonstrate the need to revisit the concept of national development and prepare an infrastructure master plan for the country over a given number of years to enable the government to better focus on the development of critical national infrastructure in an ordered manner and to remove the arbitrariness that currently pervades in the sector. Beyond the development of an infrastructure master plan for the country, faithful implementation of national development plans, leadership commitment, and absence of corruption are critical to achieving sustainable infrastructure development in Nigeria.

Major obstacles to infrastructure development

Political instability and the Nigerian civil war were the early obstacles to infrastructure development emphasized in this book. Between 1960 and 2010, Nigerians witnessed 12 government regime changes. Bouchat (2013) blamed instability in Nigeria on politics of ethnicity, religious intolerance, and poor governance. Several military coups disrupted the continuity of governance of infrastructure development. Infrastructure projects such as housing, road, rail, the Lagos "metroline" project, power plants, and steel plant constructions were either abandoned or revoked by succeeding administrations, often for no justifiable reason. Notably, political interference creates uncertainty and stifles the process of bureaucratic decision making, which, in turn, affects infrastructure development. During the Nigerian civil war (1967–1970), resources were diverted to prosecuting the war to the neglect of infrastructure development (Oyedele, 2012). Moreover, the war resulted in the destruction of the few existing infrastructures, such as the River Niger bridge in Onitsha, which had been built and commissioned two years before. After the war, there was a slow recovery effort toward rebuilding infrastructural facilities, such as roads, bridges, telecommunication, and power. The effect of the war on infrastructure development is still visible today in the war-affected areas of Nigeria.

Instability in the political environment has had direct consequences on infrastructure development in Nigeria. The situation created by decades of political turbulence still has relapsing effects on national growth and development. Political stability reinforces the interest of private sector investors in infrastructure development through public-private partnerships. Efforts should be made to ensure credible processes of electioneering and regime change to ensure political stability that could boost infrastructure development in the country.

Obstacles to implementation of government infrastructure development policies

We have seen that the implementation of government policies on infrastructure development has been hampered by funding constraints and lack of skilled local manpower and material resources. Successive administrations in Nigeria have relied heavily on foreign loans as the main source of funding infrastructure development projects in the country, and this has resulted in huge foreign debt, totaling over $40 billion in 1999 (Olaseni & Alade, 2012). By the end of 2010, the debt that Nigeria had accumulated from international borrowing to execute infrastructure development projects had skyrocketed to a worrying proportion. Revenues generated from the sale of oil are inadequate to fund all development programs, including agriculture, education, rural development, and the provision of social amenities. The government of Nigeria should expand the revenue base of the country in order to have more funds for infrastructural development, and also collaborate with the private sector to finance infrastructure development in the country.

Most material resources needed for infrastructure development in Nigeria are imported from overseas, including bitumen for highway construction, and iron and steel for bridges, railways, and housing projects. In addition, Nigeria relies heavily on foreign construction companies, such as Julius Berger and Reynolds Construction Company, to adequately execute major infrastructure projects. Human and material resources are lacking in most areas of the construction industry, particularly in road construction, telecommunications, and electrical power production. A comprehensive approach toward confronting the challenges of infrastructure development in Nigeria that takes cognizance of local manpower and materials has been advocated.

Effective and favorable government policies

The Public Procurement policy and the various privatization schemes of the Nigerian governments are considered effective and favorable in boosting the country's infrastructure development. The Public Procurement Act of 2007 stipulates measures to be followed in the awarding of contracts, especially in infrastructure development. In 1999, the Federal Government of Nigeria under the democratic regime of President Obasanjo invited the World Bank to conduct a thorough assessment of its procurement system with the goal to reforming contract award procedures, especially in infrastructure development, in order to eliminate corruption, political and personal interests, and remove obstacles that lead to government projects' being abandoned. As Ogbonna and Kalu (2012) explained, the Public Procurement Act helped to create economic efficiency and effectiveness consistent with best practices. Corruption was the main obstacle to infrastructure development in Nigeria, and the public procurement policies have helped to significantly address the problem (Anigbogu & Shwarka, 2011).

During the Obasanjo civilian administration (1999–2007), major privatization and commercialization policies were initiated in Nigeria. The sale of state-owned infrastructure agencies, such as the electric power generating company, National Electrical Power Authority (NEPA), Nigeria telecommunication company (NITEL), and the Nigerian Airways, marked a significant shift in government policy to involve the private sector in infrastructure development. While the impact of privatization on the country's economic growth may be considered beneficial to some degree (Udoka & Anyingang, 2012), there is a need for further reforms and improvement (Muogbo, 2013).

Performance and public trust

Public trust has been very low due to perceptions of poor performance in the area of infrastructure development by successive governments in Nigeria. Iroghama (2012) remarked that in Nigeria, public trust or distrust is measured largely by public perception of corruption. When the public perceive the government as working hard to manage issues relating to corruption, the level of trust increases significantly; when the public perceive the government as doing little to minimize corruption, especially in infrastructure development, the level of trust drops. Lack of accountability, especially in executing infrastructure projects, has been the main element affecting public trust in Nigeria. As Akinwale (2010) pointed out, Nigerians have developed apathy toward their governments against the backdrop of inadequate infrastructure provision. This has resulted to the gross violation of laws, leading to the prevalence of a semblance of lawless society in parts of the country.

Re-orienting bureaucrats to combat corruption in the development of infrastructure

There is ample evidence that some government officials at all levels are corrupt (National Bureau of Statistics, 2017). As Ogbuagu, Ubi, and Effiom (2014) stated, infrastructural decay can be traced to corruption, lack of accountability and transparency among bureaucratic office holders in Nigeria. For the country to make real progress in terms of infrastructure development, corrupt practices must be tamed by ensuring that the bureaucratic institutions involved in infrastructure development are made more transparent and accountable.

There is need for ethical re-orientation and accountability training for bureaucrats. Civil servants should be trained with the knowledge that in the public service, the collective needs of citizens take precedence over those of individuals. Therefore, bureaucrats should aim at making a difference in the lives of citizens by putting the interest of citizens and the 'common good' first. In the civil service, where hierarchical authority is the prevailing norm, the exercise of power must be premised on some larger set of values if it is to be effective. Those in leadership positions need to earn the respect of the employees and the citizenry. The importance placed on service values in public institutions could make the management of behavior in these institutions more pointed to service delivery. Public sector values, such as accountability, transparency, and efficient service delivery, should be made to impact on the culture of the civil service.

Public interest is served when leaders encourage employees and citizens to be deeply involved in policy and management decisions as well as provide feedbacks to ensure reinforcements in areas that have recorded good service delivery. Reinforcing feedback processes help to accelerate growth in the system. Feedback processes also ensure accountability in government. Enhanced participation by citizens and employees with its inherent feedback process could help to combat bureaucratic corruption in the civil service. In the public sector, the involvement of citizens and stakeholders should not be just a matter of convenience and efficacy; it should be built into the very fabric of public service in a democratic society.

Impact of reforms

We can conclude that economic reforms generally benefitted infrastructure development. The national development plans have been discussed as the main reform program that had the most beneficial impact on infrastructure development in Nigeria. This can be attributed to the fidelity of early post-independence leaders to the plans. A development plan can only be meaningful and successful when it is faithfully implemented, and its objectives are realized (Lawal & Oluwatoyin, 2011).

Two other reform programs – the structural adjustment program (SAP) and the public-private partnership (PPP), were specifically identified as assisting with the development of infrastructure in Nigeria. The International Monetary Fund (IMF) and the World Bank have been involved in helping the nation to restructure its economic programs. It was during the Babangida administration (1985–1993) that it experienced a major structural adjustment program. It had to devalue its currency to stem inflation and took several economic recovery measures to meet the requirements for international loans needed for infrastructure development (Taye & Dada, 2012). The SAP was a major economic reform that had severe negative consequences for Nigeria's economic growth.

The PPP program involves the public and private sectors collaborating together, towards investing and conducting business activities aimed at providing infrastructure and services in Nigeria. This emerging economic reform program has helped immensely in sourcing finance for infrastructure projects and collaborating with agencies of government in terms of skilled manpower and expertise in the infrastructure sector. There is need to improve the PPP program by developing capacity among public officers and enhancing government investments in project preparation as a necessary precondition for investment by private sector investors, especially in relation to infrastructure development in Nigeria.

Leadership style for future infrastructure development

Many citizens would agree that Nigeria as a nation needs a visionary and transformational leaders for future infrastructure development. Attributes of visionary leadership include open-mindedness, foresight, sensitivity to the needs and aspirations of people, capacity to predict the future, persistence, creativity, and strong conviction, which are all elements of transformational leadership.

Good visioning and rhetorical skills are central to transformational leadership. Essentially, this type of leadership describes how leaders can initiate, develop, and implement important changes in organizations, institutions, and governments (Bass, 1990).

The leaders and followers engage in a mutual process of raising one another to higher levels of morality and motivation (Bass, 1990; Burns; 1978). Transformational leaders do this by appealing to higher ideals and values using charismatic strategies. Bass and Riggio (2006) identified an increased awareness of the importance of the task ahead, signifying the need for great vision, teamwork, and emphasis on higher order needs, as an attribute of transformational leadership. This could be beneficial to infrastructure development in Nigeria.

Impediments to good governance of infrastructure development

From what we have seen from earlier chapters, it would appear that Nigeria's enormous oil wealth was not initially invested to build a viable industrial base and would not suffice to fund infrastructure development needs at present. It is important to find creative ways of funding such infrastructure development. A multi-pronged approach made up of budgetary resources, private investments, development and infrastructure bonds, multilateral loans, etc. should be explored.

Poor planning of infrastructure development, a dearth of skilled workers in the civil service, poor budgeting, low capital allocations and high recurrent allocations, and corruption combine to account for the poor service delivery in the infrastructure sector in Nigeria. It is recommended that conscious efforts be made to ramp up capital allocation for infrastructure development while lowering recurrent allocation by eliminating redundancies in bureaucratic institutions and cutting wastages in government.

Future areas of infrastructure development

Electrical power, transportation (roads and rails), and housing are key areas for future infrastructure development in Nigeria. With a population of about 185 million, the country needs an intermodal and integrated transportation systems that incorporates modern rail lines and highways, and water and air transportation to move the vast majority of the population, goods, and services from one place to another, and support economic growth. As Oyedele (2012) puts it, in developing countries, infrastructure refers to roads and transport infrastructures. And with 60% of the Nigerian population lacking access to electricity (Akinwale, 2010), an efficient electrical power supply is needed to improve manufacturing and provide jobs for the larger numbers of unemployed youths. It has been pointed out that inadequate electricity is responsible for the closure of many manufacturing concerns in Nigeria, and it is at the heart of the inability of the country to attain its projected GDP growth. A pragmatic approach should be adopted to improve electrical power generation, transmission, and distribution to consumers in the country by adopting an energy mix (thermal, hydro, solar, and wind) to solve the perennial electrical power problems.

Benefits of good infrastructure development

The Nigerian economy will benefit from good infrastructure networks. Good infrastructures serve as catalysts for economic growth and provide the platform for socio-political transformation. Infrastructure facilitates the production of goods and services: the supply of raw materials to the factory and distribution of finished products to end users. Good infrastructure development in Nigeria will lead to a general improvement of its infrastructure sector, thereby promoting the standard of living of the people through the enhancement of the capacity of citizens to pursue productive ventures that will lead to an increase in GDP.

Recommendations for action

The topics explored in this book have led the author to make the following recommendations:

1. The Nigerian government should revisit the concept of national development plans and restore these as a vital tool for developing infrastructure. This measure would enable the government to focus more on the development of critical national infrastructure in an orderly manner.
2. The government should reposition and strengthen institutions established to aid infrastructure development and ensure they are imbued with requisite due process practices and strong project delivery guidelines to facilitate timely implementation of projects and put an end to the trend of abandoned projects.

3 A proactive engagement against corruption in the Nigerian bureaucracy is recommended, to be accomplished by holding bureaucrats accountable to rules of procedures and processes. Corrupt public officers should be punished for proven corrupt practices. This will help to purge the bureaucracy of corruption. Bureaucratic institutions involved in infrastructure development should be made more transparent and accountable. Training should be provided to bureaucrats on the need to practice and maintain high ethical standards in service delivery.

4 The government should constantly aim to achieve political stability and security of lives and properties in order to encourage private sector investors to invest in infrastructure development through public-private partnerships. The situation created by decades of political turbulence still has negative effects on the growth and development of infrastructure in Nigeria. Foreign investors are reluctant to provide funds due to political instability. The government should develop and implement policies that will help stabilize the polity, in order to engender confidence in the system and promote private investments in infrastructure development. It is further recommended that the government engage critical stakeholders to address the twin issue of political instability and insecurity, which could pave the way for increased private sector investments in infrastructure development in Nigeria.

5 A major reform of the infrastructure sector, leveraging on local construction materials and human resources, should be carried out to make the sector attractive to private sector investors. The ever-rising population of Nigeria, currently about 185 million people, should provide a ready market that would patronize privately built infrastructure, whether it is tolled roads, private electricity distribution companies, private transportation companies, or private water distribution companies.

6 To address the issue of funding constraints, it is strongly recommended that the government look beyond its lean budgetary resources and explore creative ways of tapping into private sector finances. Funding mechanisms such as raising infrastructure bonds for projects that are self-sustaining and could be paid off over a period, and other different private finance initiatives, should be tapped into to minimize funding constraints. Local sourcing of materials should be integrated into the designs of infrastructure projects in Nigeria to eliminate the need for imported construction materials. A deliberate policy should be put in place by the government to patronize local companies and help them develop business capabilities that will enable them to carry out many of the construction contracts.

7 Research for this book has indicated that roads, power, and transportation infrastructure are the key priority areas for future infrastructure development in Nigeria. While power is vital to manufacturing and entrepreneurial activities, for a country of 185 million people,

a good transportation infrastructure network is needed to move persons, goods, and services from one part of the country to another. It is recommended that the government should have as its infrastructure development priority the production of adequate electrical power and transportation. The government should leverage on collaboration with the private sector to unleash the creative potentials of Nigerians and help promote sustainable economic growth and development. This would help to build public trust and promote good governance in Nigeria.

8 Finally, it is recommended that accountability and transparency be firmly entrenched in the processes guiding infrastructure development in the country, and that a communication strategy be instituted whereby citizens are briefed periodically on critical national infrastructure projects. This will lead to the creation of a citizens' awareness forum, and this may restore public trust in the government.

Implications for social change

We have uncovered several important social issues. To begin with, it is evident that inadequate funding, lack of planning, political instability, lack of political will, and corruption are some of the challenges facing the governance of infrastructure development in Nigeria. Nigeria has not been able to break the cycle of economic inadequacy and underdevelopment since gaining independence in 1960. Inadequate infrastructure is at the root of its economic problems: it would benefit immensely from the provision of a good and adequate infrastructural network. This network would make the distribution of goods and agricultural produce easier and more efficient, and could reduce the prices of goods in retail outlets. A good network of roads would help to minimize accidents and human deaths on Nigerian highways and contribute to increased GDP due to improved travel times and quicker turnarounds for businesses. If railways, airports, and seaports are developed as advocated in this study, the transportation constraints that Nigerians experience in major cities, such as Lagos, Kano, and Port Harcourt, could become a thing of the past.

In addition, the development of the communication and electrical power components of the economy would have a significant social impact on the people of Nigeria. Nigeria is currently plagued by an erratic and unreliable supply of electrical power. This is a major setback to the overall growth and development of its economy. Nigerians spend a huge amount of their personal incomes providing their own electricity using generators. The health hazards associated with pollution emissions from these generators cannot be ignored. The government ought to prioritize the problem of electricity in Nigeria. A stable supply of electricity and the completion of abandoned steel plants and rolling mills in the country will lead to the massive employment of Nigerians in the manufacturing sector and help unleash their creative potentials. Businesses in the manufacturing sector will also ramp up manufacturing activities and help raise the country's GDP. No economy can succeed without a dependable steady supply of electrical power. On the same token, business development and social interaction are hampered by poor communication networks. Developing this aspect of Nigerian infrastructure would promote business and better living for its people.

Conclusions

There has been infrastructure development in Nigeria between 1960 and 2015, but a huge gap exists in its development. Progress has been made in the development of transportation infrastructure, such as the construction of roads, airports, and seaports. These accomplishments have significantly improved the infrastructural needs of the nation. However, they have not been adequately maintained, leading to early dilapidation; routine maintenance is critical for sustainable economic growth and development. National development plans in Nigeria contributed immensely to infrastructure development in the past and ought to be developed, refined, and sustained in the future policies and plans of the government. This is critical to the future progress of infrastructure development in Nigeria. Political instability, religious intolerance, terrorism, and poor governance are impediments to infrastructure development and should be addressed by the government.

For Nigeria to reach a reasonable milestone in the development of infrastructure, requisite funds and adequate local material, as well as trained human resources should be provided. Inadequate funding was a major constraint in infrastructure development over the past 55 years. The government has a responsibility to adequately fund infrastructure development and so must increase the amount of money set aside for construction projects. Government efforts at boosting infrastructure development will be an exercise in futility if the corruption that permeates the contract procurement process and the bureaucracy are not addressed. This is at the heart of the infrastructure development crisis in Nigeria. The negative impact of bureaucratic corruption on infrastructure development is monumental. Nigeria needs leadership that is committed to fighting corruption through strengthening government institutions that are engaged in infrastructure development are used strictly for that purpose. This is a challenge to the political leadership of the future in the governance of infrastructure development in Nigeria. This measure is vital for building public trust and maintaining good governance.

The government cannot accomplish the huge task of providing adequate infrastructure for the nation alone. Private sector participation is crucial to realizing this goal. The public-private partnership initiatives currently embraced by private investors in Nigeria should be intensified, especially in infrastructure development. The government should provide incentives to attract local and foreign investors to develop infrastructure projects in Nigeria.

Nigeria needs visionary and transformational leadership to achieve sustainable infrastructure development. Ultimately, the future governance of its infrastructure development should be in the areas of transportation (roads, railways, airports, seaports, and waterways) power, education, portable water supply, health facilities, housing and manufacturing. Ultimately, infrastructure development in Nigeria has had moments of progress between 1960 and 2015, but a lot more effort by political leaders is required for it to reach satisfactory levels of growth and development, and stand shoulder to shoulder with other developed nations.

Bibliography

Adenugba, A. A. (2013). Good governance and accountability in Nigeria's development dilemma. *Mediterranean Journal of Social Sciences, 4*(2), 777. Retrieved from www.mcser.org/journal/index.php/mjss/article/view/267

Akinwale, A. A. (2010). The menace of inadequate infrastructure in Nigeria. *African Journal of Science, Technology, Innovation and Development, 2*(3), 207–228. Retrieved from www.ajstid.com

Anigbogu, N. A., & Shwarka, M. S. (2011). Evaluation of the impact of the public procurement reform program on combating corrupt practices in public building projects delivery in Nigeria. *Environtech Journal, 1*(2), 43–51. Retrieved from www.google.com

Awamleh, R., Evans, J., & Mahate, A. (2005). A test of transformational and transactional leadership styles on employees' satisfaction and performance in the UAE banking sector. *Journal of Comparative International Management, 8*(1), 3–19. Retrieved from http://journals.hil.unb.ca/index.php/JCIM

Bass, B. M. (1990). From transactional to transformational leadership: Learning to share the vision. *Organizational Dynamics, 18*(3), 19–31. doi:10.1108/0143773 0410538671

Bass, B. M., & Roggio, R. E. (2006). *Transformational leadership* (92nd ed.). London: Routledge.

Bedell-Avers, K., Angie, A. D., Eubanks, D. L., & Mumford, M. D. (2009). Charismatic, ideological, and pragmatic leaders: An examination of leader-leader interactions. *The leadership Quarterly, 20*, 299–315. Retrieved from www.sciencedirect.com/science/article/pii/S1048984309000770

Bouchat, C. J. (2013). *The causes of instability in Nigeria and implications for the United States.* Retrieved from www.strategicStudiesInstitute.army.mil/

Bryant, S. E. (2003). The role of transformational and transactional leadership in creating, sharing and exploiting organizational knowledge. *Journal of Leadership and Organizational Studies, 9*(4), 32–44. doi:10.1177/107179190300900403

Burns, J. M. (1978). *Leadership.* New York, NY: Harper & Row

Federal Government of Nigeria (2010). The millennium development goals (MDGs) report, Retrieved from www.undp.org/content/dam/undp/libray/MDG/english/MDG

Iroghama, P. I. (2012). Trust in government: A note from Nigeria. *International Journal of Academic Research in Economics and Management Sciences, 2*(1), 258–267. Retrieved from www.hrmars.com/admin/pics/838.pdf

Lawal, G., & Tobi, A. (2006). Bureaucratic corruption, good governance and development: The challenges and prospects of institution building in Nigeria. *Journal of Applied Sciences Research,* 2(10), 642–649.Retrieved from www.aensiweb.com/jasr.html

Lawal, T., & Oluwatoyin, A (2011). National development in Nigeria: Issues, challenges and prospects. *Journal of Public Administration and Policy Research,* *3*(9), 237–241. Retrieved from https://academicjournals.org/journal/JPAPR/article-abstract/C6BD9F816095

Marcellus, I. C. (2009). Development planning in Nigeria: Reflections on the national economic empowerment and development strategies (NEEDS) 2003–2007. *Journal of Social Sciences, 20*(30), 197–210.

Muogbo, S. U. (2013). Impact of privatization on corporate performance: A study of selected industries in Nigeria. *International Journal of Humanities and Social Science Invention,* 2(7), 81–89. ISSN (Online): 2319–7722. Retrieved from www.ijhssi.org/papers/v2% 287% 29/Version-1/K0271081089.pdf

National Bureau of Statistics (2017). National corruption report. Retrieved from https://www.unodc.org/documents/data-and-analysis/Crime-statistics/Nigeria/Corruption_Nigeria_2017_07_31_web.pdf

Ogbonna, A. C., & Kalu, L. U. (2012). Public procurement reform in developing countries: A critique of the real estate context in the Nigerian case. *International Journal of Management Sciences and Business Research,* 1(8), 65–77. Retrieved from www.ijmsbr.com/

Ogbuagu, U., Ubi, P., & Effiom, L. (2014). Corruption and infrastructure decay: Perceptible evidence from Nigeria. *Journal of Economics and Sustainable Development,* 5(10), 20–27. Retrieved from www.iiste.org/Journals/

Okekeocha, C. (2013). A case study of corruption and public accountability in Nigeria. A Practicum Paper for M.A. Degree. Kennesaw State University.

Okonjo-Iweala, N. (2012). *Reforming the unreformable: Lessons from Nigeria.* Cambridge, MA: The MIT Press.

Olaseni, M., & Alade, W. (2012). Vision 20:2020 and the challenges of infrastructure development in Nigeria. *Journal of Sustainable Development,* 5(2), 1–14. doi:10.5539/jsd.v5n2p63

Onolememen, M. O. (2015). The impact of leadership on the governance of infrastructure development in Nigeria (Doctoral dissertation). Walden University, Minneapolis, MN.

Oyedele, O. A. (2012). The challenges of infrastructure development in democratic governance. *Constructive Economics and Management,* 1(6119), 1–15. Retrieved from www.fig.net/TSOIC

Rogger, D. (2014). The causes and consequences of political interference in bureaucratic decision-making: Evidence from Nigeria. Conference paper. Retrieved from www.bsg.ox.ac.uk/sites/blavatnik/files/documents/04.%20Dan%20Rogger%20The%20Role%20of%20Politicians%20-%20paper.pdf

Taye, O. O., & Dada, M. O. (2012). Appraisal of private sector involvement in infrastructure development in Lagos, Nigeria. *Mediterranean Journal of Social Sciences,* 3(2), 399–412. doi:10.5901/mjss.2012.v3n2.399

Udoka, C. A., & Anyingang, R. A. (2012). The effects of privatization on economic growth on Nigeria: 1979–2007 in retrospect. *International Journal of Economic Development, Research and Investment,* 3(2), 25–35. Retrieved from www.icidr.org/

United Nations (2007). *Public governance indicators: A literature review.* Retrieved from http://unpan1.un.org

Index

Note: **Bold** page numbers refer to tables and *italic* page numbers refer to figures.

www.ingramcontent.com/pod-product-compliance
Lightning Source LLC
LaVergne TN
LVHW021109300926
849160LV00009B/655
9781032175362